P9-EMP-581

NATIONAL GEOGRAPHIC DIRECTIONS

ALSO BY BARRY UNSWORTH

The Songs of the Kings

Losing Nelson

After Hannibal

Morality Play

Sacred Hunger

Sugar and Rum

Stone Virgin

The Rage of the Vulture

Pascali's Island (published in
  the United States as *The Idol Hunter*)

The Big Day

Mooncranker's Gift

The Hide

The Greeks Have a Word for It

The Partnership

C·R·E·T·E

C·R·E·T·E

BARRY UNSWORTH

NATIONAL GEOGRAPHIC DIRECTIONS

NATIONAL GEOGRAPHIC
Washington, D.C.

Published by the National Geographic Society
1145 17th Street, N.W., Washington, D.C. 20036-4688

Text and photographs copyright © 2004 Barry Unsworth
Map copyright © 2004 National Geographic Society

All rights reserved. No part of this book may be reproduced or transmitted in any form or by any means, electronic or mechanical, including photocopying, without permission in writing from the National Geographic Society.

Library of Congress Cataloging-in-Publication Data

Unsworth, Barry 1930-
    Crete / Barry Unsworth
        p. cm. -- (National Geographic directions)
    ISBN: 0-7922-6643-9
    1. Crete (Greece)--Description and travel. 2. Unsworth, Barry,
1930---Travel--Greece--Crete. I. Title. II. Series.

DF901.C8U58 2004
949.59--dc22

                                                              2003068871

One of the world's largest nonprofit scientific and educational organizations, the National Geographic Society was founded in 1888 "for the increase and diffusion of geographic knowledge." Fulfilling this mission, the Society educates and inspires millions every day through its magazines, books, television programs, videos, maps and atlases, research grants, the National Geographic Bee, teacher workshops, and innovative classroom materials. The Society is supported through membership dues, charitable gifts, and income from the sale of its educational products. This support is vital to National Geographic's mission to increase global understanding and promote conservation of our planet through exploration, research, and education.

For more information, please call 1-800-NGS LINE (647-5463), write to the Society at the above address, or visit the Society's Web site at www.nationalgeographic.com.

Interior design by Melissa Farris

Printed in the U.S.A.

To my grandchildren

CONTENTS

C·R·E·T·E

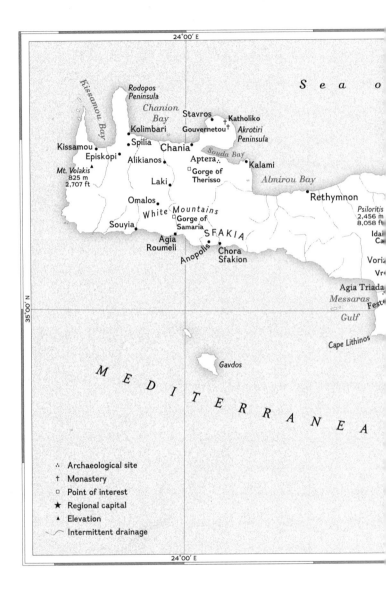

Sea *o*

Kissamou Bay

Rodopos
Peninsula

Chanion
Bay

Stavros • • Katholiko
Gouvernetou †
Akrotiri
Peninsula

Kolimbari

Kissamou •

Spilia

Chania •

Souda Bay

Episkopi •

Alikianos •

Aptera ∴

• Kalami

Mt. Volakis ▲
825 m
2,707 ft

Laki •

□ Gorge of
Therisso

Almirou Bay

Omalos •

White Mountains

Rethymnon

Psiloritis
2,456 m
8,058 ft

Souyia •

□ Gorge of
Samaria

SFAKIA

Idai
Ca

Agia
Roumeli

Anopolis

Chora
Sfakion

Voria

Vr

Agia Triada

Messaras
Festi

Gulf

Cape Lithinos

M
E
D
I
T
E
R
R
A
N
E
A

Gavdos

∴ Archaeological site
† Monastery
□ Point of interest
★ Regional capital
▲ Elevation
⌒ Intermittent drainage

35°00′ N

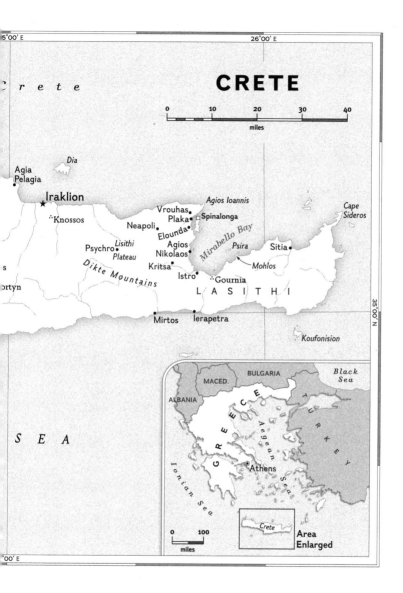

26°00′ E

r e t e   **CRETE**

0   10   20   30   40
miles

Dia

Agia
Pelagia

★ **Iraklion**

Knossos   Vrouhas   *Agios Ioannis*
                    Plaka   □ Spinalonga   *Cape*
              Neapoli   Elounda   *Sideros*
                          Agios
Psychro *Lisithi* Nikolaos   *Psira*   Sitia
        Plateau   *Mirabello Bay*
s   Kritsa   *Psira*   Sitia
  Dikte Mountains   Istro   *Mohlos*
rtyn   Gournia
                                        L A S I T H I

                    Mirtos   Ierapetra

35°00′ N

Koufonision

                    MACED.   BULGARIA   *Black*
              ALBANIA   *Sea*
                                                  T
                                    G   E   U
                              R   E   R
                              E   *Aegean*   K
S E A   E   *Sea*   E
                              C   Y
                              Athens

                    Ionian
                    Sea

0   100   *Crete*   **Area**
miles   **Enlarged**

CHAPTER ONE

CAVES *of* ZEUS

AND

HOUSES *of* CHRIST

We decided to go in early May. We packed swimming things, but didn't much expect to swim. The sea is too cold at this time of year, for all but the most hardy. A Cretan rarely ventures into the water before July. The sun of May is hot, though, and needs to be treated with respect. My wife, Aira, and I intended to do a lot of walking—Crete is one of the best places for walking that I know of—so sun hats and dark glasses and fairly stout footwear came high on the list of priorities.

The sky looked soft as we came down, but there was nothing soft about the land. One sees the bare bones, boulder-strewn fields with cleared areas, a reddish brown in color, almost terra-cotta, and the distant range of the Lefka Ori, White Mountains, their crests covered with snow. Landing, we were enfolded in the special blend of ancient past and slightly ramshackle present that seems a particular property of the island.

For the Greeks of a later time, Crete was the most venerable and ancient place imaginable. It was where everything began. The first herders of sheep were Cretan, the first beekeepers and honeymakers, the first archers and hunters. These last were the mythical Kouretes, sons of Earth, who attended on the infant Zeus. Since everything began here, it was also the birthplace of Zeus, the father god of the Greeks.

The legend has it that he was born in a cave near the present village of Psychro, high in the Dikte mountains on the southern edge of the Lasithi plateau in eastern Crete. His mother, Rhea, came here to give birth to him in secret, so as to save him from her husband, Kronos, ruler of Heaven, who, having been told that a son of his would supplant him, routinely devoured all his off-spring. Rhea presented him with a stone instead, and in his cannibal haste he swallowed it without looking too closely. She then repaired to Crete and had the baby, leaving it in the care of the Kouretes, who in addition to their other achievements were the inventors of the armed dance, clashing their bronze weapons against their shields to drown out the baby's cries and so prevent

Kronos from discovering the trick that had been played on him and eating this one too.

For the kind of writer I am, stories like this make a strong appeal. I often use the past, sometimes the remote past, as a setting for my fiction. It's a matter of temperament, I suppose, but I find this distant focus liberating, clearing away contemporary clutter and accidental associations that might undermine my story, and allowing me to make comparisons with what I see as the realities of the present. So it's a sort of fusion, an interaction of past and present. This is probably one of the reasons why I have always liked Crete, the quintessential land of such fusions.

The exploration of this remote cavern in the mountainside, conducted in the first spring of the twentieth century by D. G. Hogarth, then director of the British School in Athens, had for both of us, when we read about it at home before leaving, all the drama and romance of early archaeology on Crete, carried out by men and women endowed in equal measure with classical learning and a passionate spirit of inquiry. There were no roads, only rough tracks through the mountain passes. The workmen and their equipment—stonehammers, mining bars, charges of gunpowder—had to be transported on mule back. Leonard Cottrell quotes from Hogarth's own account in the issue of the *Monthly*

Review, which appeared in the following year. He describes his first sight of the cave, with its "abysmal chasm" on the left-hand side: "The rock at first breaks down sheer, but as the light grows dim, takes an outward slope, and so falls steeply still for two hundred feet into an inky darkness. Having groped thus far, stand and burn a powerful flashlight. An icy pool spreads from your feet about the bases of stalactite columns on into the heart of the hill."

The upper-right-hand chamber had already been broken into and robbed several times over, but the lower, deeper one had never been explored. The blast charges soon cleared away the scattered boulders that had blocked entry to generations of would-be plunderers. The labor force, increased now by the recruitment of female family members—Hogarth believed that the presence of women would make the men work better—began to dig, descending steeply day by day into the darkness of the cavern until only the dots of light made by their candles could be seen in the distance.

Now comes the miraculous discovery. One of the workers, as he was setting his candle in the narrow crack of a stalactite column, caught sight of a shine of metal—there was a blade wedged there. When drawn out it proved to be a bronze knife of Mycenaean design. There was no way it could have got there by accident:

Someone, in the remote past, had brought it as an offering to some god or gods.

Encouraged by this, the party began to search among the crevices of these immeasurably ancient limestone columns that gleamed with moisture in the light of their candles. In the days that followed they found many hundreds of objects: knives, belt clasps, pins, rings, miniature double-headed axes, wedged in slits in the stalactites, brought down by devotees into these awesome depths some four thousand years before. Hogarth had no doubt that he had come upon the original birthplace of Zeus. "Among holy caverns of the world," he wrote, "that of Psychro, in virtue of its lower halls, must stand alone."

I suspect that what might have been harder for Hogarth to imagine than those long-ago worshipers was the impact that late-twentieth-century mass tourism was to have on these sacred grottos, hitherto undisturbed for millennia. The birthplace of Zeus has struck the popular fancy. Buses run from points all over the north of the island, from Chania to Ágios Nikolaos, following the coast road, turning inland at Neapoli, toiling up the winding road to the Lasithi Plateau. Vociferous and sometimes importunate guides wait at the foot of the trail that leads up to the cave. There are numbers more at the entrance, armed with flashlights and a great deal of Cretan inventiveness and storytelling verve. They can distinguish among the stalactites the niche where the baby Zeus was bathed and the hollow where his cradle was laid. In spite of all this, in spite of the confusion of flashlights and the echoes of conflicting commentaries, when you are in the depths of the cave and look back toward the hazy nimbus of light above you, a certain awe descends. This patch of sky is what the newborn Zeus, destined to be father of gods and men, first opened his eyes upon.

Numerous others, however, argue that the true birthplace of Zeus is the Idaian Cave, on the edge of the Nidhi Plateau below the summit of Mount Ida, modern Psiloritis, which at 8,058 feet is the highest point on Crete and capped with snow for most of the year. The name means "the forest," pointing to the fact that these slopes were once thickly wooded. The Idaian Cave has a long history as a cult place, going back to Bronze Age Crete and lasting into Roman times. According to tradition the philosopher Pythagoras visited the cave and offered a funeral sacrifice to Zeus there.

I am a great believer in the power of the imagination, especially when tuned to the past. But it can falter sometimes, and mine falters when I try to picture Pythagoras as a flesh and blood person standing in a cave, praying. He is nothing but an abstract principle for me and a source of frustration into the bargain. We met while I was still in short trousers (boys wore short trousers in those days), when I was required by the geometry teacher to prove Pythagoras's theorem concerning right-angle triangles, something I never succeeded in doing throughout my school days.

At five thousand feet above sea level, the setting is spectacular, but the cave itself is shallow and rather mediocre as Cretan caves go, lacking the dramatic cavernous depths of its rival. The issue has not been settled yet at the academic level—the arguments are erudite but inconclusive. I would be quite content to leave them in that state forever and suspend judgment, but Aira, always anxious to solve problems before passing on, was glad to hear that a sort of practical solution has been reached, at least in the eyes of the Tourist Board and the respective local populations. On the basis that two excursions are better business than one, it has been established that the Diktaian Cave is where the god was born and the Idaian Cave where he passed his infancy, suckled by wild animals.

Dark, underground places, the limestone spine of Crete is riddled with them, associated from earliest times with orgiastic practices and worship of the divinities of earth. And here already the Cretans demonstrate their difference. For the Greeks of the mainland, Zeus was a sky god. He ruled from the zones of the upper air, he was the thunderer, the cloud gatherer. What was he doing skulking in caves? But the Cretans are extremely tenacious in argument and greatly gifted in the art of having the last word. Since they saw Zeus as a fertility god, who died with the dying year and was reborn with spring, since they already had his birthplace, why not claim his tomb as well? This they proceeded to do, establishing it on the highest summit of Mount Juktas, south of Knossos, rousing great fury among those who believed the god to be immortal. Among these was the sixth-century B.C. poet and miracle priest, Epimenides, himself a half-legendary character, a fragment of whose invective has survived, translated by Rendel Harris and quoted by Costis Davaras in his book on Cretan antiquities:

> *The Cretans carved a tomb for thee, o Holy and High,*
> *Liars, noxious beasts, evil bellies.*

I intoned this to Aira as we stood among the spring flowers looking up at the fabled summit, and she suffered my pomposity with her usual good grace. Epimenides was a Cretan himself, which lends added force to his words. St. Paul the Apostle refers to this verdict seven hundred years later, in his Epistle to Titus, by tradition first bishop of Crete. This judgment of them by a prophet of their own is true and well founded, the Apostle says, and goes on, "Wherefore rebuke them sharply, that they may be sound in the faith."

But the shopkeeper in Chania with whom Aira and I stopped to chat while he was standing in his doorway enjoying the morning sun saw matters quite differently. He invited us inside, offered us coffee, showed us with a mixture of pride and guile around the shelves of hand-painted ceramics. Some had designs drawn from classical mythology, and prompted by this, he gave us his own version of the Zeus story. The Greeks of Athens had stolen the god, changed him out of all recognition, and made him their own. And this was because in the wars between Crete and Athens, temporarily and with the help of traitors, the latter had been victorious. What better way of marking a victory than by taking over the gods of the defeated? The Minoan palaces of Knossos and Festos had been devastated by fire at just that time; what more could be needed by way of proof?

I watched his face as he talked. Clearly these events were as real to him as if they had happened the day before yesterday. Cretans love stories. Their island has been inhabited for eight thousand years at least, time for a lot of stories, time for that long process of creative embroidery in which myth and legend and history intermingle, interweave, become inextricable.

Not surprising that disputes among scholars and archaeologists should concern caves. There are over two thousand of them on the island. The four great massifs that spring from the sea with astounding suddenness to form the mountainous core of Crete are all composed of limestone. The acid content in rainwater dissolves it, makes tiny furrows and hollows in the surface, in which the water gathers. Over vast spans of time, sinkholes develop, the limestone becomes riddled with fissures and crevices, and the constant sculpting by the water carves out caverns below the surface, underground chambers, some simple, some complex, with galleries at different levels, sometimes reaching into the heart of the mountains. Stalactites form, the water gathers into streams and pools. In these lightless tunnels and caverns and labyrinthine watercourses three billion years of life on our planet have produced a huge variety of crawling, swimming creatures, blind and colorless, perfectly at home.

Caves and rock shelters are intimately bound up with Crete's history from very earliest times. They formed the first shrines and cult centers, provided refuges from pirates, hideouts for bandits and revolutionaries in the uprisings of the eighteenth and nineteenth centuries, and for partisans during the Second World

War. They were sometimes the scenes of terrible atrocities carried out against the rebellious local population. Xan Fielding, visiting one such cave in the 1950s near the village of Vaphes in the eastern part of the White Mountains, saw a plaque set in the rock face commemorating the 150 men, women, and children of the village who had taken refuge in the cave and were put to death by suffocation in August 1821 on the orders of two Turkish pashas, Resit and Osman. The story goes that their presence in the cave was betrayed to the Turks by the crying of a child.

We had already decided to start by visiting some caves. It's an excellent way of getting to know Crete, since they are found everywhere, and there is invariably something of interest to see on the way. And Chania, on the northwest coast, probably the oldest and certainly the most attractive city on the island, is a good place to start from.

We took the road westward from Chania to Kolimbari at the base of the Rodopos peninsula, and then turned south toward Episkopi, along the valley of the Spiliakos River. It was a relief to get off this coastal road, especially the stretch nearest Chania. Running alongside the sea, with only the narrowest of strips dividing it from the shore, it has been subject to drastic tourist development on either side, a more or less continuous ribbon of hotels, vacation apartment houses, beach cafés, supermarkets, and souvenir shops, jumbled together in a way that we found chaotic and oppressive.

In compensation, the tourist-clogged road served to make the hills inland, once reached, all the more serene and lovely. The road follows the valley through groves of wonderfully luxuriant olive trees. You see these best in May, when the trees are a mass of yellow flower rifled by bees, or in late autumn, when the fruit darkens. The foliage is a denser green, and the branches have a more spreading habit than those of the western Mediterranean; it is altogether a more lordly tree, clothing the hillsides right up to the crests. The oil from these olives, any Cretan will tell you, is like no other anywhere else on Earth. There is something about olives that seems to bring out regional chauvinism. At home in Umbria we have our own olive trees and make our own oil—which naturally we consider to be the best anywhere to be found. The Tuscans think exactly the same about theirs, as do the people of Apulia. In fact, a lot depends on habitual taste and methods of cultivation. The best oil comes from freshly handpicked olives. If the nets are kept spread under the trees for several days and the olives gathered from the ground, which is the practice in southern Italy, the oil will be more acid. At least, that's the view we take in Umbria.

The cave we were making for is on a hill above the village of Spilia. It is best approached on foot, a walk of just a few minutes, but before taking the track upward we went to see the Church of the Panagia on the edge of the village, with its air of slumbering calm and its fine fourteenth-century frescoes and its wide terrace giving a view of the sea and the headland of Akrotiri. These village churches on Crete have an air of complete and utter tranquility. They are swept and clean, the beveled red roof tiles are repaired or replaced, the walls are whitewashed, there are well-tended gardens all around. Often enough you see no one, but the care of some hand is everywhere evident, a blend of the devotional and the domestic, cats and fig trees and icons all mixed in together. Never a formal garden, no sense of elaboration, no concept of dignifying the space around, but a gardener's care for plants for their own sake, and for what they might yield, the lemon, the fig, and the almond growing among trees planted only for their flowers or the beauty of their shape. So it didn't surprise us to see chickens running about, and a goat or two.

But the symbolism of Christianity, dramatic, tragic, extremely undomestic, intervenes when you least expect it. On the way up toward the cave a rough track leads off to a steep rise with a life-size wooden image of Christ on the Cross at the summit. A stony slope, the crucified figure outlined against the sky, and it is Calvary we are looking at.

The Cretan maquis, the scrub of the hillsides, is less green than that of Umbria and Tuscany, which is the region I am used to, but it is not pale. The earth is reddish, and as spring advances into summer the vegetation dries to russet in the fierce sun, and there are colors of orange and purple in it—fire colors. In evening or morning, when the sun is low in the sky and falls more obliquely on the hillsides, the scrub glows with a soft burnish, flame-colored, forming a landscape almost too beautiful to be quite believed in. From March to May or early June, a profusion of wildflowers clothes the whole expanse: malva, borage, sumptuous thistles, large, pale yellow marguerites, asphodel, orchis. Later the aromatic shrubs take over, warmed into dizzying scent by the sun: cistus, savory, thyme, sage, broom, and many others.

This flowering from the stony soil in a country of relentless summers seems almost miraculous, precarious by virtue of its own tenacity, something dearly achieved. Especially this is so with the more delicate-seeming flowers, thrift, pale pink convolvulus, petromarula, the tiny exquisite flowers resembling speedwell but darker blue that thrust the perfect shape of flower and leaf from the stones of the path under our feet. Blind growth, of course, subject to its own laws; but it is hard not to feel it the result of some caring, nurturing agency, some quality of devotion similar to that we felt at work in the surroundings of the church below.

Reaching the grotto of Agios Ioannis Xenos, St. John the Stranger, we felt this presence again. A large cave on various levels, with twisting passages, sudden openings into sunlight, small secondary chambers resembling chapels, where there might be a table draped with a fringed cloth, a geranium in an earthenware pot, candles to be lit by the faithful, icons here and there, propped against the rough rock of the walls.

St. John the Stranger was a hermit who lived in this grotto—and died here—in the eleventh century. Almost certainly a succession of holy men had inhabited the place before him. Built into a cave adjoining the main grotto is a small basilica, roughly vaulted and walled. An altarpiece, covered with a plain cloth, a brass candlestick with the stub of a candle in it. All around, on walls and vault, is evidence of frescoes painted at the time of the saint, now largely effaced by the long years of damp and decay. There is the same sense here of something dearly achieved, achieved against the odds, the order, the patient care in this lonely place so long deserted, mainly visited now by the curious and skeptical—like us; something stubborn and unyielding in it too, this care, something of the spirit that kept Cretan identity intact through centuries of grinding oppression. The frescoes seem to express the same indomitable spirit. Despite the ruining of time, the lineaments of humanity have not been lost; here and there the dark expressive faces are almost untouched. One of the three kings survives, leaning forward, proffering his gift; the head of the Virgin is still inclined in the icon posture of submission.

Less than a mile south from here, in the direction of Episkopi, a footpath leads off the road through woods to the tiny chapel of St. Stephen. With its whitewashed walls shaded by overhanging oak trees, it seems at the same time remote from the landscape and perfectly at home in it. Even in midsummer you are likely to find this tiny jewel of a church deserted. The frescoes here date from the period immediately following the expulsion of the Arabs from Crete in A.D. 961.

The Arab conquest and occupation of the island was one of the darkest periods in Cretan history. Originally from Cordoba in Spain, a band of Saracen adventurers, who had been driven from their base in Alexandria in A.D. 823, landed on Crete, led by their emir, Abu Hafs Omar. They defeated the Byzantine rulers and subjugated the island piece by piece, destroying most of the existing towns in the process. The invaders were interested only in plunder. In the 150 years of their rule, they turned the island into a slave market and pirate base, subjecting the Cretans to a degrading servitude, preying on the neighboring coasts, and pillaging the islands of the Aegean. During this period Crete was cut off from Byzantium and so from her co-religionists and the whole world of Christendom.

When the Saracens were finally defeated and Crete restored to Byzantine rule—which was to last until the Venetian invasion of 1204—there was a great sense of liberation throughout the island. The beauty and vitality of the church frescoes of this period give evidence of this, and we see a striking example in this tiny, isolated chapel of St. Stephen, where, after a thousand years of time and chance, the face of St. Mark the Evangelist, complete in every detail, still arrests the visitor with its power and delicacy. Aira took a photograph of this marvelous face and then worried in case it would be too dark, though in fact it came out beautifully. Of course, photographs never do justice to our experience. They can't contain the complex of impressions that made the experience so memorable. But memory too suffers from a similar sort of necessary simplification. A visual image is never purely visual; it depends on the feelings and sensations of the moment, elements beyond our power of recall.

Closer to Chania, on the eastern side, the Akrotiri peninsula thrusts out to sea like a helmeted head on a

Near Episkopi: The fresco of St. Mark the Evangelist in the chapel of St. Stephen

long and bony neck. Here again there are caves to see, and for those visitors who don't mind a bit of scrambling, it offers a rich and rewarding experience—and a great deal more besides.

Following the roads on the eastern side of the peninsula will bring you to the monastery of Agia Triada, surrounded by cultivated fields and luxuriant olive groves—all the work of the monks. This is one of the best preserved of Cretan monasteries, built in the Venetian style, the stone of its walls a beautiful reddish sand color that glows in the sun as if radiating its own light. Unlike the great majority of monasteries on the island, it still functions as a community, but the outlying buildings are dilapidated and more or less abandoned—goats and cats are the main tenants nowadays.

Perhaps because such communities, and the life of work and prayer that goes with them, are dwindling and under threat of extinction, they exercise a strong fascination for many of the people who come to Crete. It was only nine o'clock in the morning when we made our visit and still fairly early in the season, but we found four buses parked outside and a sizable crowd in the precincts of the monastery. The monks' cells were locked and silent, and we supposed their occupants were out working in the fields. The abbot sat at one side of the ticket desk, watching the people come and go.

There was olive oil on sale, made by the monks themselves on their own press, bearing the label of the monastery. The income from tourism is devoted to reconstruction and repair and general upkeep, but it is difficult to imagine that this alone can restore the fortunes of the monastery. And certainly it can't redress what is of course the main problem: the steady decline in the monastic spirit and way of life, the shortage of candidates.

All the same, the glories of the past are very much in evidence, though much has had to be rebuilt in the course of the monastery's violent history. The main church, which stands in the center of the courtyard, was sacked by Turkish irregulars engaged in suppressing the Cretan uprising of 1821, in which many of the monks took part. After everything of value that was detachable had been carried off, the church was set alight. According to eyewitness accounts, the fire was so devastating that afterward the church resembled a limekiln. So intense was the heat that the stone blocks of the building turned to lime, and the iron bars supporting the chandelier, and the bronze of the chandelier itself, melted like wax. Naturally, none of the original church decorations could survive this. But the monks returned and set to work. The present rood screen is an exact replica of the original astonishing proliferation of carved

The monastery of Agia Triada

forms, patterns of foliage and birds and beasts and human figures, with the gaze of prophets and saints in the icons, somber and intent and of utmost simplicity, seeming, as always, to repudiate the opulence of decoration in which they are set.

The best way to go on from here, still on the way to our cave, is on foot, at least if one wants to get the feel of the landscape. But preferably not in the middle hours of the day in summer: The Cretan sun can be fierce and there is little shade. We took a detour roughly two miles farther north, toward the sea, to another monastery, that of Gouvernetou. The road to it is spectacularly scenic, running at first through a landscape of scattered rocks and wild olives, a setting that seems, in its beauty and desolation, to be awaiting some imminent miraculous event, then following the twists and turns of a ravine between faces of rock and scrub rising sheer on either side.

In early summer these slopes are ablaze with flowering gorse, the bushes a rounded shape, keeping close to the ground. Black goats clamber at impossible angles—most often one hears the tinkling of their bells without seeing the animal. The kids sound an anxious lonely bleating when they feel too far away from the mother. This, and the fugitive sound of the bells, and the murmur of the bees as they move among the spreads of thyme and rockrose, are all the sounds there are in these hills.

The monastery of Gouvernetou is older than Agia Triada and more austere in its architecture, with fortress-like walls enclosing the beautiful cruciform church. In the seventeenth century, during the final years of Venetian rule, it was one of the wealthiest monasteries on the island, with huge estates and a thriving community of monks. But it suffered losses under the Turks, and in the great uprising of 1821 it underwent the same fate as Agia Triada—and all the other monasteries on this peninsula of Akrotiri, in greater or lesser degree. Many of the monks were massacred and the monastery was sacked. Today it feels remote and isolated. Strange tormented faces are carved on the stone columns of the church facade, an unusual feature, more resembling the grotesqueries of Western Romanesque architecture than the more formal Orthodox tradition. Souls in pain? Demons excluded from the holy precincts? It is difficult to tell. A disheveled, sad-looking monk sells us some postcards. There are only four monks left in residence.

Now for our cave. From the northern end of the monastery square a rocky footpath winds gradually down in the direction of the sea. A few minutes' walk brings you to a large cavern with daylight at its mouth and strange effects of shadow in its recesses. This is the very ancient cave of Arkoudiotissa, or Arkouda, once sacred to the goddess Artemis, who was worshiped here in the form of a bear—*arkouda* in modern Greek. And indeed there is a bear here, or the effigy of one, a stalagmite formation hunched in the dimness, leaning forward with lowered head over a stone-built cistern. Water drips steadily from overhead into the cistern. You are never likely to hear another sound so clear and distinct.

Many hundreds of thousands of slow-dripping years have gone to form this crouching creature. He was already a very old bear when Artemis was brought from Asia to be incorporated in the pantheon of the Greeks. Not difficult to see why this cave would become the center of her cult—the bear was sacred to her. But inside this same cave is another shrine, belonging to another faith: a chapel dedicated to Mary Arkoudiotissa and consecrated to the Purification of the Virgin. Mary inherited the bear, so to speak, just as the Orthodox Church inherited the ancient gods and absorbed them into its rituals.

Nikos Psilakis relates the local legend according to which the bear was alive once and used to come to the cave and drink up the water in the cistern, so that the monks of Gouvernetou went thirsty. They never caught the bear in the act of drinking, but when they went for water they always found the cistern dry. So one day they waited in hiding. But when the bear appeared it was so huge that they were panic-stricken. They couldn't see anything, the bear shut out the light. One of them began asking the Virgin to intercede. Even as he prayed, the bear, caught in the act of drinking, was turned to stone.

The path goes on descending, more steeply now, with steps cut in the rock. Half an hour or so brings you to the ruins of another monastery, this one with its own cave, and a deeply impressive one—the church itself is built into a cavern in the hillside. This is the Katholiko monastery, also known as the Monastery of St. John the Hermit, generally thought to be the oldest on Crete. It was abandoned by the monks three hundred years ago because of repeated pirate raids.

Whether, in its long history, Crete has endured more suffering through piracy than it has inflicted is a question that can have no final answer. The totals, on both sides, are beyond arithmetic. The Cretans practiced piracy even in prehistoric times. By Homer's day they were famous for it, raiding coasts far and near. The practice does not seem to have been frowned upon. In the fourteenth book of *The Odyssey,* Odysseus, passing himself off as a Cretan, relates his exploits as a pirate so as to gain the respect of his hosts, boasting of the nine raids that he made and the haul of plunder that fell into his hands.

However, in later times the island suffered terribly from Muslim corsairs raiding from their bases in North Africa. This was particularly so after 1204, when the Byzantine sea power was destroyed in the course of the Fourth Crusade and they were no longer able to patrol the coasts. Most of the best land lies on the coastal plains and so is peculiarly vulnerable. Oliver Rackham and Jennifer Moody, in their book on the making of the Cretan landscape, draw attention to the extreme fluctuations of population in these regions, which remained abandoned and uncultivated for long periods out of fear of pirate raids. The Venetians, during the centuries of their rule, maintained a fleet of galleys on the island whose main purpose was to protect the coasts against these marauders. But the situation did not greatly improve until the Turkish conquest in the seventeenth century, when the Christian islanders and the Muslim pirates became fellow subjects of the Ottoman Empire. This must be accounted one of the benefits brought about by Turkish occupation—they were extremely few.

Katholiko is dramatic and spectacular in its desolation now, with its church cut into the rock, its monumental stone bridge spanning a deep chasm. Built to join the monastery buildings, the bridge joins only ruins now, arching proudly over a wilderness of rock and shrub. From the track above you can trace the

Remains of Katholiko monastery

course of the streambed, dry in the summer months, following the gorge to the sea, which is visible from here, a gleam of water, a narrow inlet, a stony beach— the track of the pirates.

The sides of this wild valley are dotted with caves, places of earlier worship perhaps—or earlier refuge. The cave of the hermit, in which he is said to have lived and died, lies just above the monastery, tunneling deep into the hillside, following the course of an underground stream. The saint's grave is here, but one needs a flashlight to see it. It is said that, enfeebled by his privations and ascetic way of life, he could no longer walk upright but stooped so much that it looked as if he was going on all fours. A man out hunting mistook him for an animal and wounded him fatally with an arrow. He was just able to crawl back to his cave, and there he died.

There is always a story, especially on Crete. It can sometimes seem that the whole island is a patchwork of stories, from primal myth to heroic legend to the embroideries of local gossip. But there have been some discoveries here that defy all attempts at narrative elaboration, so bizarre and surreal do they seem. The fossil bones of dwarf mammals have been found in Cretan caves, an elephant smaller than a bullock, a pig-size hippopotamus, a deer with legs shorter than a sheep's.

The large mammals that were the ancestors of these beasts migrated to Crete some time after the end of the Miocene period, four million years ago, probably by following one of the land bridges that came and went, connecting Crete with adjacent mainlands. When these bridges were finally submerged, the migrants found themselves stranded on a mountainous island. They had no enemies to worry about, but the areas of standing water and marshland were steadily dwindling. They had to adapt or die. Smallness was the solution; without predators they didn't need to be so big and food supplies went further. By the time they encountered their first carnivores, in the shape of Neolithic man, they had forgotten how to run away.... After studying the bones, scientists have come to the conclusion that these dwarf hippos could climb. We are not far away here from the country of the centaur and the unicorn.

Returning to Chania on the western side of the peninsula via Stavros, one of the best beaches on the island, a slight detour brought us to the Venizelos graves, the stone-built tombs of Eleutherios Venizelos and his son Sophocles. Venizelos is Crete's most famous son, regarded by many as the greatest of modern Greek statesmen for his role in freeing Greece from Turkish occupation and extending her territories in the early years of the twentieth century.

The graves are simple, unpretentious, lacking in pomp. From the heights you get commanding views of the city of Chania and the great sweep of the bay beyond, as far as the tip of the Rodopos peninsula. But the tombs were not situated here for the view alone, marvelous as it is. Once again, in a way that seems peculiarly Cretan, history and legend interweave. On this spot, in 1897, Venizelos, in the course of leading an insurrection against the Turkish rulers, raised the flag of a united Greece in defiance of the European powers, who still had not consented to the union of Crete with Greece. The flagpole was smashed by a shell from one of the ships in the bay below, but the Cretan rebels took up the flag and kept it flying, braving the enemy fire. The story goes that this so impressed the sailors that they broke into applause, abandoning the guns. It is also related, and in parts of the island still believed, that a Russian shell damaged the roof of the Church of Elijah the Prophet, and that this sacrilegious act brought divine retribution—the ship exploded the very next day, for no apparent reason....

CHAPTER TWO

OLD *is* NEW

in CHANIA

Chania is the best place to start when you first come to Crete. It is well placed for seeing the west of the island, which is the region least frequented by visitors, since the coast lacks beaches large enough for tourist development. In recompense you get a sense of remoteness and timelessness here, passing through unspoiled villages, exploring virtually deserted coves, overshadowed constantly by the spectacular presence of the White Mountains, the most imposing range on the island, with a score of peaks that rise to around eight thousand feet, capped with snow from December to June.

The old quarter of the city and the harbor are entirely captivating. In the maze of narrow streets

Chania: the Venetian harbor

are endless discoveries and surprises, a complex pattern of what has been altered out of all recognition, what has been modified, and what has survived untouched since the Venetians took it from the Genoese in the early years of the thirteenth century, changed its name from Kydonia to La Canea, set about establishing the mansions for their notables that still line the harbor, and constructed the tremendous walls that made the city a bulwark in defense of a maritime empire that was to endure for close on five centuries. The Venetians were great wall builders. You see their work all over the island, with the Lion of St. Mark carved like a trademark over arches and lintels. The massive walls they built to defend the harbor of Chania still stand, as do many of the mansions, now often ramshackle and partly in ruins, or converted to new uses,

apartment houses or banks or hotels. During our time in Chania, we stayed in one such hotel, the Casa Delfino, a beautifully converted former palazzo still preserving its paved courtyard, where we had breakfast, its stone staircases, and elegantly arched windows.

Standing on the old harbor front on a summer evening, facing toward the open sea, with the sun sinking beyond the barren headlands to the west, you are looking at what the earliest inhabitants of this very ancient city saw, the same tints of bronze and fire red and gold that shift across the sheltered water, the same tremulous and fugitive reflections, the same gathering softness in the sky as the light fades. Crete is a harsh land in some ways, unyielding, but its nighttime skies in summer are marked by this indigo softness.

Colors of things, effects of light, these may defy time, but materials do not. The dome of the Mosque of the Janissaries is concrete now, but it still crouches impressively beside the water, with its cluster of lesser domes, a warm biscuit color in the harbor lights, symbol of Ottoman conquest, looking across at the works of its predecessor and rival for empire, still evident in the narrow arched windows and elegant balconies of the houses that the defeated Venetians left behind them.

In general, it is the Venetians who have left their mark on this city rather than the Turks, but the Janissaries were dreaded in their day. This famous corps, the shock troops of the Ottoman Empire in the days of its supremacy, has no parallel in the annals of military history. It was formed in the fourteenth century from Christian slave children, who were converted to Islam, sworn to celibacy, and trained in blind obedience to their commanders and the ruling sultan. In later times, when the central Ottoman power was weakening, discipline was relaxed, they were allowed to marry and granted the privilege of enrolling their children in the corps—the best fed and best paid in the army. Levies of Christian youths ceased after the end of the seventeenth century. By the beginning of the nineteenth the Janissaries were completely out of control, a law unto themselves, a public nuisance and a danger to their own rulers. By tradition they used to gather around their cooking cauldrons to take counsel; when these cauldrons were overturned, it was a signal of rebellion—they would no longer eat the sultan's food. The atrocities they committed on the Cretan population—who, as always, resisted the foreign yoke—were notorious, probably worse than anywhere else in the Ottoman-controlled Greek lands. They were finally destroyed in 1826, shelled out of existence by regular troops of the Turkish army under the command of the formidable Ibrahim Pasha, known by the nickname of Kara Jehennem, "Black Hell."

Their mosque in Chania is used now for exhibitions and displays of various kinds. From here to Angelou Street, the old harbor is lined with restaurants, and just about every one of them has a man posted on the pavement outside to solicit the custom of passersby. Anyone who makes this circuit in the summer months will receive instruction in the inventiveness, the inveterate self-defining faculty, of human beings in general and Cretans in particular. The men outside these restaurants, whether young or old, stout or lean, handsome or homely, are aiming at the same thing: They all want to see you seated at one of their tables scanning the menu. But they have adopted a variety of ploys in accordance with temperament. One will assume an earnest manner, even

A *Chania street*

slightly aloof. He doesn't want to tell you how good the restaurant is, only that it has been there since 1961—a fact also proclaimed on a huge placard overhead. Forty years, it seems, is a long time for a restaurant to exist, in this city which has existed for millennia. Another will be loud and direct and boisterous, like a barker at a fair. Another will sound a wistful note as you pass: Sooner or later, today or tomorrow, you will succumb, you won't be able to help yourself. Another waxes confidential, buttonholes you, man to man: Let me tell you something about this place that perhaps you don't know.... Then there is the action man, who blocks our path, thrusts a menu into our hands.

The Cretans, like their compatriots on the mainland, have a great flair for marketing. They make choosing a restaurant resemble shopping in some vast bazaar. And a sort of bazaar it is, though marked with a curious sameness in the midst of profusion. Cretan restaurant food can be very good and the helpings are generous, but—as opposed to the style of those whose task it is to inveigle you inside—there is a certain lack of variety in the main courses. Bream or mullet grilled or baked, mutton grilled or stewed, these form the traditional choices. Depending on the restaurant, variety can be found in the range of snacks known as *mezedes,* which are often very good indeed, typically consisting of miniature spiced meatballs and sausages, small triangular-shaped cheese or spinach pies, vine leaves stuffed with rice and pine nuts, *tzatziki* (chopped cucumber, garlic, and yogurt), little saucers of mashed chickpeas or white haricot beans in lemon juice. Still in the exuberant spirit of the bazaar or treasure house, all these items, however small, will be chalked up separately, as if they were main courses, forming long lists on the big slates standing outside. Go inside and you are likely to find them all on one tray. Some restaurants, by no means all, offer Cretan specialties, done as they really should be done: a fish soup called *kakavia* flavored with onion and lemon, a dish called *horta,* which is a judicious mixture of wild greens, some of them bitter and some sweet, gathered fresh from the hillsides, boiled and served cold, with olive oil and vinegar. This may sound simple, but it isn't. When the flavors are blended as they should be, it is superb.

Another very good reason for starting in Chania is that it is distant from the great Minoan palace sites in the central part of the island, remains of a unique and splendid civilization that reached its high point around 1500 B.C. These must be visited, of course—they are what large numbers of people come to Crete for. But there is a lot to be said for approaching from the edge, beginning with the humbler remains that have been unearthed here. Most people, in Minoan times, after all, did not live in palaces, any more than they do today.

Two Minoan sites are being excavated at present in Chania, close together on Kanevaro Street, in the district known as Kastelli, the high ground overlooking the harbor on the eastern side. This is the oldest part of the town, generally believed to be the site of ancient Kydonia, which is the name the Byzantines knew the city by in early Christian times.

Looking at these bare traces, hardly above the level of the ground but demonstrating an order that could never be thought accidental, bearing the unmistakable touch of human design, one has the usual sense of the muteness, the sadness of ruined habitations. The people who lived here were members of a Bronze Age society more advanced than any that had gone before, and any that were to come after for a thousand years. They belonged to the time called by archaeologists the New Palace period, when Minoan civilization was at its most dynamic, when the palaces of Knossos and Festos were being rebuilt after a cataclysmic earthquake, devastation on a scale that would have put an end to a society less vital. The jewelry the well-to-do among these people wore, the textiles and ceramics they used in their houses, have never been surpassed in quality of workmanship and beauty of design. They were not Greeks and their language was not Greek. We call them Minoans, but what they called themselves we don't know. The name we use was given to them by Sir Arthur Evans, the great archaeologist, who named the people after their legendary ruler, King Minos. Evans was the first man to carry out extensive excavations in Crete. He and others worked on sites throughout the island in the early years of the last century, uncovering an entire civilization that had lain unsuspected below the earth and rubble for thousands of years. Together with Schliemann's work on the site of ancient Troy a little earlier, it was one of the greatest enterprises in the history of archaeology.

The buildings whose ruins we peer at through the fence on Kanevaro Street were twice destroyed by fire—perhaps more often, there might have been a long cycle of destruction and rebuilding. The first time known to us was around 1450 B.C., when this part of the town was consumed in a great conflagration mysterious in its origins. Minoan sites throughout the island show traces of violent destruction and the scars of fire dating from this time. Natural disaster or the work of invaders or a combination? This is an argument that still goes on.

Poignant evidence that the fire came without much warning is a jar found on the site, containing a quantity of burned peas. A loom was also found, scorched but still recognizable, bringing to mind the peaceful domestic round of the people who lived here, soon to be engulfed. They came back again, in the course of time, from the places where they had found shelter or taken refuge, returned with that tenacity we still see today in the victims of earthquake or flood, who come back to the places they know and painfully rebuild them, seeking to recover the life they had before, which will never again, of course, be quite the same.

Three centuries later these houses were destroyed by fire once again, probably by Greek tribes from the Balkans equipped with iron weapons. This time there seems to have been no recovery, no return—at least no rebuilding: Any who came back must have lived among the ruins. But the fire, devastating as it must have been, brought with it one unforeseen and startling benefit. On this site, baked by the fire and so accidentally preserved, clay tablets were discovered bearing the written language of the people, what came to be called the Linear A script, pictograms of various plant and animal products. These, in spite of devoted efforts, have not yet been fully understood, but they point to a system of economic administration far in advance of anything else in the world of the Mediterranean at that time.

Then came the further, sensational discovery of tablets of a later date, written in a different script, called Linear B. In the early 1950s, after long efforts by such scholars as Michael Ventris and John Chadwick, this was deciphered and shown to be an early form of Greek, proving the presence here of Mycenaeans from the mainland, who by then had become the dominant power. No other site has been so far discovered containing examples of both scripts. What more lies below this hill of Kastelli can only be conjectured; most of the ancient city of Kydonia has not so far been excavated and is perhaps unlikely to be so now. The streets and houses and shops and office blocks have covered it over.

But these scripts, so accidentally discovered, have a value symbolic as well as historical. In this dark weave of violence and destruction, in which both human agencies and acts of God, as they are called, have played their part, there are lighter threads running through; and among them—perhaps chief among them—is human language, human writing. The desire to communicate is the desire to save, to preserve from destruction. This is a paradox that has always accompanied our story and it finds a vivid example here, in these obscure remains. Our own age is just as barbarous, or more—more, certainly, if the criterion lies in capacity for destruction. One hopes the archaeologist of the future will find evidence, in the ruins of our society, of this same saving desire to understand our fellows.

Kanevaro is an ordinary street, with ordinary activities going on: a few stores, a bar, a workshop, people passing—and a fenced-off area where other people lived their ordinary lives three and a half thousand years ago. Such conjunctions are present everywhere on the island, and in Chania, with its long history of human habitation, they spring out at you at every turn.

Still in Kastelli, not very far from the Minoan remains, there is a ruined monastery. Rising high above the broken arches of the cloister and all the tumbled debris of this ancient place of worship, where Byzantine priests once intoned their liturgies, there is a huge placard with a notice: ROOMS FOR RENT WITH BATHROOM AND SEA VIEW. For a wild moment it seems that some Cretan entrepreneur is offering to let ground space among the venerable vaults of the narthex and the weeded wasteland all around. A sea view there would be, certainly, and rooms enough, though roofless. The bathroom would be more problematic. But drawing nearer, you see that a house has been built inside the shell, a cunning combination of ancient stone and modern bricks and mortar. This is the Monastiraki Pension, lodging of undeniable character. The people of the island were for centuries the poorest of the poor. Now, for some of them, the past has turned to gold under the Midas touch of tourism.

The past snatches at you in the names of the streets and restaurants too, but it is the mythical past now. There is the Talus Bar, named after the bronze giant who was given by Zeus as a present to Europa, to be the guardian of her island of Crete. He was said to be the last survivor of the third race of men, after those of gold and silver, people fashioned in bronze, a ferocious race who destroyed themselves in endless warfare. Talus patrolled the cliffs of Crete and threw huge rocks down at any intruders he saw. He was kept alive by a single vein, closed at the ankle with a bronze pin. In the end he was betrayed by the sorceress Medea, who lulled him with promises of immortality and then pulled out the pin....

Then there is, inevitably, a Minos Street, named after the legendary king of Crete, who had the labyrinth of Knossos constructed as a home for the monstrous Minotaur, unnatural offspring of the union of his queen with a bull. The Minotaur, who, as the name suggests, was half royal prince, half bull, fed on human flesh. From Athens there came an annual tribute of youths and maidens to be sacrificed to him.

Close by is Ikarus Street, named for was the son of the great artificer Daedalus, who built the labyrinth. Father and son were kept imprisoned in this same labyrinth by King Minos. Daedalus made wings for them both out of wax and feathers, and the pair embarked on a daring escape plan. But Ikarus forgot his father's warning not to fly too near the sun. The wax melted and the young man went plunging down into the sea near the island of Samos.

These myths of Crete are among the most ancient we know and have a special quality that makes them stand out among the complex ramifications of Greek mythology. They have a darkness and splendor about them that is essentially tragic. They are stories that have shaped the imagination of the Western world.

Certainly they have shaped mine, from a very early age. The first book—the first real book—that I can remember possessing was called *Tales from Olympus,* a collection of Greek myths with beautiful color plates, or so I thought then, to illustrate them. I think I was about four at the time and better equipped to admire the pictures than read the text. And, of course, the stories were toned down and poeticized in a way that was thought then to be suitable for children—perhaps the toddlers are tougher now. The treachery and murder so prevalent in Greek myth had been softened. But the characters of the gods and goddesses, and their dealings with humans, came through in all its drama and has been with me ever since.

On this visit I was particularly aware of the mythological associations. I know I kept exclaiming at the names and launching into long explanations. This must have seemed a bit excessive to Aira, though she didn't say so. Not much before leaving I had written the final paragraphs of a novel set in Greece on the eve of the Trojan War, and in an effort to understand the worldview of the people of that remote time I had done a lot of background reading: Homer, Greek tragedy, works on prehistoric religion and mythology. So my mind was still full of it. Now, three months later, it's fading already, as I contemplate a new novel set in a totally different period. It's similar in a way to studying intensively for an exam. For a while you know everything, you are a walking encyclopedia, you bore friends and strangers alike with unasked-for information. Then, mercifully, it starts to get vaguer. In my time I have been a temporary expert on eighteenth-century sailing ships, medieval drama, the career of Horatio Nelson. To mention but a few.

In any case—because Crete so much sharpens one's sense of the past, because the associations we form are so swift as to seem unconscious, because of the ruggedness of the island, present-day sights can carry one back in imagination to remotest times. The harbor front at Chania, the light fading, a group of local soccer fans in red-and-white-striped shirts, some wearing a sort of jester's cap and bells in the same colors, holding aloft a huge red banner bearing the emblem and name of the club. They gather around the banner in a massed group, they take it by the corners and lay it on the ground. They sway their bodies forward and back, chanting a name in devotional unison, raising their arms above their heads, all together, in one concerted movement. The word they are chanting is indistinguishable. The name of a football star or a name of a god? They throw flares that land sizzling on the water. From some soundless smoke bomb in the midst of them, thick swirls rise up, showing ashy pink in the harbor light. The chant continues, and the rhythmic movements of the bodies forward and back, and for a while we are in the presence of a spirit that goes back to a time before Greek and Venetian and Turk, back to the earliest settlements here, to a people primitive and fearful, with jealous divinities to be propitiated.

Sometimes the clashes of period are more ironic, more like sly jokes. Outside a store on Halidon Street in Chania is an exact copy in plaster of *La Bocca della Verità,* the Mouth of Truth, a stone disc with the face of a Roman river god carved on it, set in a wall in the portico of the Church of Santa Maria in Cosmedin in Rome. The Romans used these discs as drainage lids or sluices for regulating the water system of the city, but this particular one was retrieved and placed in the wall of the church, probably sometime in the late Middle Ages. A popular superstition grew up around it, no doubt encouraged by the authorities, as it made the task of intelligence gathering easier. According to the legend, anyone suspected of heresy or conspiracy was obliged to put a hand into the stone mouth. If innocent, nothing happened; if guilty, the hand was bitten off. In short, this was a medieval lie detector.

This simulacrum, on a busy street in Chania, strikes a note of incongruity almost comic. To convey

Chania: La Bocca della Verità

a sense of remoteness and antiquity, the Cretans use an image that belongs to a time much less remote than the far reaches of their own past—the Romans are of yesterday by comparison. Between pizzeria and car-rental agency, with his abundant tresses and luxuriant beard designed to simulate the flow of water, an expression of open-mouthed consternation on his face, this minor god watches the people and the traffic pass. Above his head there is a slot for coins, and above this the words HAND ANALYSER. Now and again people stop before him, insert a euro, press a button for the desired language, and put their hands into the mouth, palm uppermost. The river god prints out a character analysis. The oracle has been computerized. The analysis will not contain anything to trouble or disturb. People chuckle but in some way perhaps believe it, and the euros clink. Even in such standard-ized versions of ourselves we cling to the notion of our own uniqueness.

It is above all in the Archaeological Museum, on the same street, that the layers of history are most apparent. Of course, any museum will have this effect—it is the effect museums aim at. But this particular collection is housed in a building that is in itself an eloquent testimonial to fusions of past and present. This was originally the Church of San Francesco, built by the Venetians, once one of the island's most imposing churches, now deconsecrated and lacking the soaring bell tower that once symbolized its virility.

The bronze figurines and terra-cotta sarcophagi and Hellenistic and Roman sculptures and Minoan ceramics are displayed in the chapels and along the sides of the nave. Roman mosaics depicting the pagan loves of Bacchus and Ariadne are laid out on the floor of this Catholic church in the place where the altar once stood and the Eucharist was performed.

Ariadne too has her place in the myths of Crete. She was a daughter of Minos, and when the hero Theseus came to the island, along with the other youths and maidens sent as tribute from conquered Athens to be sacrificed to the Minotaur, she fell in love with him. After he had killed the monster in the heart of the labyrinth where it lived, he was able to find his way out again by means of a ball of thread Ariadne had given him, one end of which was attached to the entrance. Theseus took her away with him as he had promised, but abandoned her on the Aegean island of Naxos, where she was discovered in tears by the god Bacchus—or Dionysos, as he was called by the Greeks. She became his consort and after her death he set her in the sky as the constellation Corona Borealis.

The Minotaur was half man, half bull, a strange hybrid creature. There is much about the ancient Cretan bull cult that we don't know. The huge quantity of clay figurines of bulls on display in the museum is distinctly mysterious. Of small size and crude workmanship, they have been excavated in great heaps in the surrounding region. Perhaps offerings to Poseidon as god of fertility and virile force. Certainly much cheaper to offer than real ones ...

We come upon a showcase with finds from the tomb of one Sossima, who died in childbirth around 300 B.C. Scraps of gold thread from her funeral dress, necklaces for the afterlife, the gold coin that was placed in her mouth to give to the boatman Charon so that he would ferry her across to the Underworld. These remains of an arrested life convey the same sadness as the jar of burned peas in the Minoan house, though ten centuries separate them in time.

In the small courtyard outside we hear the strains from somewhere nearby of a Brahms symphony. A venerable mulberry tree shades the whole area, planted probably during the Ottoman occupation—the Turks were fond of mulberry trees and planted them all over the island. There is a beautiful Turkish fountain with grooves at the base for ritual washing before entering the mosque. Across from this a stone lion, faceless and eroded but still with mane and haunches and an inscription below, still readable: EVANGELISTA MEUS.

The Lion of St. Mark, symbol of Venetian power, the Mohammedan ablution grooves, the romantic German music, make for a kind of blended effect, a sense of the merging of times and places that can become addictive for those who spend time on the island.

Walking westward along Zabeliou Street, following the line of the harbor, one gets the essential feeling of the old city. At the end of Moschon Street is what remains of the Renieri Gate—the Renieri were one of the ruling Venetian families. The line of the arch is still intact, a whole culture of elegance and propriety in a few yards of curving stone. On the lintel above the gate the Renieri coat of arms can still be made out. Not far away is the palazzo the family once owned. This was later the property of a Turkish official who screened off the courtyard and separated it from the street beyond to protect the ladies of his harem from the gaze of passersby. The chapel which formed part of the original palazzo—the only remaining family chapel in Chania—still stands, or at least a narrow section of the facade does, squeezed between buildings on either side, with its rose window and Gothic doorway. The inner courtyard of the palazzo, where the Renieri once took their ease and later the jealously guarded ladies of the harem strolled, has undergone a third metamorphosis. It is now the excellent Sultana

Restaurant, where you can enjoy your raki and mezedes and watch the stars come out overhead.

We might easily have missed this restaurant, which would have been a pity. Near our hotel, we walked past it several times a day and every time the owner tried to lure us in, but for one reason or another we didn't succumb until we were almost at the end of our stay in Chania. There was a singer and two men with bouzoukis at a corner table, playing quietly together—it seemed they were making the music for themselves rather than as a tourist attraction. Cretan folk songs at first, full of sorrow—or so it sounded to our untutored ears. But then they went on to some of the songs of Theodorakis, which I remembered from my first stay in Athens, forty years ago now. You heard them everywhere in those days, in the streets, in tavernas, from car radios. They were an expression of popular feeling, many of them political in tone, closely associated with the Left. When, some years later, there was a military coup in Greece and the country was taken over by a junta of colonels, one of the first things they did was to ban the music of Theodorakis. For anyone returning to Athens during this period, as I did, the silence in the streets seemed like mourning. When the regime collapsed, the songs came flooding back again. Songs are like legends: Whether old or new, they are difficult to suppress.

CHAPTER THREE

CRETAN GORGES *and*

OTHER MATTERS

Chania is an addictive sort of place with its ancient harbor front, the maze of streets behind, the constant varying of the light as one moves toward or away from the open water, the sense of long-established human presence, almost exuded from its walls. One can spend many days here, closely similar but never quite the same, in a sort of ruminative pottering. It is almost a shock to emerge from the town with its cafés and gift shops and kiosks with foreign newspapers, and find the unyielding Cretan landscape awaiting you.

Two hours by road—and a very tortuous and vertiginously winding road it is—southward from Chania into the White Mountains, brings you to the gorge of

Samaria, which has been a national park since 1962. At eleven miles it is famous as the longest gorge in Europe, and it is perhaps the most spectacular on the island—though about this there are differences of opinion; Crete is home to a hundred gorges at least, all with their own distinctive qualities and their own advocates. However, Samaria is certainly the one most popular with visitors. Many thousands of people set off to walk the length of it, a mistake in some cases: It can be a taxing hike, steep in places, stony underfoot, and much of the way exposed to the sun. Broken limbs, heart attacks, cases of exhaustion are not uncommon.

The route to the gorge takes you past the village of Alikianos, in the heart of the district known as Portokalachoria, "The Orange Villages," where the best oranges on Crete—and therefore, Cretans would say, the best in the world—are grown. These villages lie in the foothills on the western side of the range, where the mountains descend more gradually, stretching bony knuckles toward the Chania plain. In the valleys formed by the spreads between the knuckles, the orange groves are bunched thickly together, a separate, secret-seeming world of dark green and gleaming gold.

But one is never far, wherever one goes on Crete, from the island's turbulent past. It was here at Alikianos, among what are now peaceful orange groves, that what came to be known as the Kandanoleon wedding massacre is believed to have taken place. The uprising against the Venetians headed by George Kandanoleon in 1527 is one of the great stories of Cretan resistance, the usual compound of fact and heroic legend. He had his base at Meskla and at the high point of his fortunes controlled most of western Crete. One day, for reasons which have remained obscure, he called in person at the house of a high Venetian official named Francesco Molino and proposed the marriage of his son Petros with Molino's daughter. A harebrained proposal on the face of it, in view of the arrogance of the Venetian rulers and their detestation of this rebel chieftain and of the Greek Orthodox faith to which he belonged. However, the proposal was accepted with seeming pleasure. The wedding took place at the Molino house. Kandanoleon was accompanied by several hundred of his followers. Molino had invited fifty guests from Chania. A hundred sheep and oxen were slaughtered for the occasion. The Venetian plied his visitors with wine, and by sunset they were well on the way to being drunk and incapable. Then a rocket was fired, signal for the approach of a force of Venetian cavalry and infantry that had been waiting nearby. The Cretans by this time were too far gone either to resist or flee. They were overpowered, bound hand and foot, and kept captive through the night. At daybreak Molino hanged Kandanoleon and the bridegroom with his own hands. The members of the more prominent families were killed on the spot or marched off in chains to be galley slaves. The remaining captives were hanged in four separate groups in different regions of western Crete. The rebellion was then suppressed with utmost brutality by a man called Cavalli, who was sent from Venice with special powers. One of his initiatives was to offer a pardon to any who made a token submission by exhibiting to the authorities in Chania the head of his father or brother.

This was the last in the long chain of Cretan revolts against Venetian rule. Whether Kandanoleon was seeking to consolidate his own power base or—more idealistically—trying to bring an end to the suffering of his people are questions unlikely to be answered now. Xan Fielding, to whose account of the massacre I am indebted, inclines to set his action down to *philodoxia,* a word difficult to translate, a quality between ambition and vainglory, an excessive desire to cut a good figure, always a Greek—and Cretan—failing.

The ruins of the Molino mansion are still there, overgrown with weeds and long abandoned. On the lintel above the entrance the Latin motto can still be made out: *Omnia Mundi Fumus et Umbra* (All the Things of the World are Smoke and Shadow), a saying which was to apply with particular force, in the next century, to Venetian dreams of conquest and empire.

After Alikianos the road to the Samaria Gorge branches eastward and winds steeply up into the mountains. The scenery is stupendous, the sheer drops and precipitous bends amazing and alarming. One passes above the village of Laki, a mesh of white and green, overlooking the valley of the Vrisi. Laki is the birthplace of Micheli Yanneri, another famous Cretan hero and rebel who distinguished himself by his resistance to Turkish occupation in the nineteenth century.

Something of the wildness of those days still persists here. The intractable spirit that made these mountain people such difficult subjects for a succession of invaders still shows in their attitude to local regulation and control. The road signs have to be changed from time to time—they are used for target practice and get riddled with bullets.

Life has always been hard in these regions, and the inhabitants are reared in a tradition of independence and endurance. They are people of great spirit and generous hospitality and implacable vindictiveness. They make good friends but extremely bad enemies; injuries are neither forgiven nor forgotten—and the conditions of village life in these remote areas has always bred injuries, real or imagined. Disputes over grazing rights and sheep stealing and insults to womenfolk still go on, as they have for a thousand years at least. Not infrequently they lead to blood feuds, and these are not easy for the authorities to stop, first because the authorities themselves are not greatly trusted and second because fear of revenge keeps people from talking. Feuds of this kind can run through generations and on occasion in the past took the form of pitched battles. Villages were sometimes abandoned altogether as the population sought safety elsewhere. This is not the case now, of course, but deadly feuds still occur. One between two Sfakian families, which broke out in the 1940s, lasted half a century and claimed at least 150 lives before peace was made.

Last inhabited place before the entrance to the gorge, and last chance of getting anything to eat or drink for several hours, is the village of Omalos, at the center of the plateau which bears the same name. A desolate region this, getting on for four thousand feet above sea level, snowbound in winter, often marshy in spring, especially if the snows melt early. You are in the heart of the White Mountains here, with the high peaks rising all around you.

A mile or so farther on, at the edge of the plateau, the road ended, and the gorge opened before us. The sun had hardly risen, there were swirls of mist, and it was cold. For those who are set on the walk, it makes sense to arrive in early morning, to allow plenty of time for covering the distance. This means that the journey up is often done in half-light, a blessing for the more nervously inclined, as the hazards of the road are not fully realized. On arrival we found at least a dozen buses already there, with walkers clambering out, beginning the descent in a steady stream, without waiting for the sun to bless their enterprise. One of the many incongruities of mass tourism that Crete presents is that in this unlikely place, among these lonely and majestic mountains, many hundreds of people of all ages and conditions congregate each dawn throughout the summer months. The gorge is closed in winter, but by mid-May buses from all over the island converge here.

Better to wait for the sun. It should be numbered among the wonders of the world to stand here on this last piece of level ground and see the sun strike through the early mists, irradiate the peaks of Mt. Volakis to the south, and cast a glow on the sheer walls of the amazing chasm that yawns open before you. We stood for some time, full of wonder, I trying not to acknowledge to myself that I was cold, Aira—who has no time for stoical pretenses—openly shivering. Then the last of the mist thinned away and the sun came through—even thus early in the year and thus early in the morning, unmistakably a southern sun with an immediate, caressing warmth. As if this were somehow an invitation, we began our descent to levels the sun would not reach for some hours yet. With appalling abruptness the ground falls away—at our very feet, it seemed—and goes plunging down. You descend three thousand feet in the first hour of walking. Two million years it has taken to make this great slice in the land. Some remote convulsion, a buckling and heaving as the tectonic plates shifted and scraped together, and the first cracks were made. Then the long, infinitely slow process of forcing the edges apart, the acid rainwater, the splitting and fragmenting of rock as temperatures changed. Then the mountain torrent that found the cleft and cut it deeper and deeper.

As we follow the rough stone track down toward the bed of the stream—much shrunken in summer but still running and sounding—with the bare limestone mass of Volakis rising before and the looming bulk of Mt. Pachnes to the east, we progress from rugged isolation to a gentler climate, the result of warmth and shelter lower down and the presence of water. Instead of descending into the apocalyptic pit, we descend to birdsong and flowers. From the vulture to the chaffinch,

The gorge of Samaria

from the riven pine with its limbs trammeled in rock to the graceful lines and spreading green of the Cretan maple and the vivid flowers of the oleander bushes growing above the stream.

Just before the descent begins to level out there is a small chapel dedicated to St. Nicholas, and grouped around it are some of the most splendid cypresses one is ever likely to see. The cypress is the main woodland tree of these western mountains and quintessentially Cretan in its toughness and tenacity and the amazing variety of forms it can take in response to the widely differing climatic conditions on the island. It can root in a crack in the rocks in the driest and most torrid of places; it can stand the whipping of the wind and the scouring of the ice and endure for many hundreds of years. There are cypresses at the tree limit of the White Mountains growing at an altitude of over five thousand feet. They keep low to the ground, rarely exceeding two meters in height, and they live long—some of them are a thousand years old. Those surrounding the chapel have had shelter and water, and they are huge, among the biggest in Europe, with girths it would take six men to embrace. Some of them rise to heights of 160 feet and more. To get a full idea of this, bear in mind that the Colosseum of Rome is not much more than a dozen feet higher.

The path gradually levels out toward the streambed and the going gets easier. We were now more at liberty to study the walls of the chasm—sometimes looking as if they had been sliced with some unimaginably huge butcher's cleaver—that rise on either side. Every layer of rock is delineated as precisely as if the lines had been drawn with a ruler, bands of green, purple, and gray limestone alternating with a whitish, flintlike rock known as chert. Perhaps a hundred million years of geological history here, from the time that the limestone mass that was someday to be Crete was thrust out of the sea.

At times on this walk a feeling akin to dread seizes one, the scale is so enormous, the stream that runs through the cleft so narrow and bubbling and innocuous-seeming. At this season, using stepping-stones, you can cross and recross it without getting your feet wet. Could such a streamlet really have made this mighty ravine? In winter, when few see its rages, it becomes a torrent, perilous to anyone caught between the walls.

The dread intensifies—or perhaps it could better be described as a feeling of intense wonder—when the sheer faces of the gorge draw together, a little past the halfway mark, at what are called the *Sideresportes,* the "Iron Gates." The walls soar almost vertically on either side to a height of fifteen hundred feet and seem almost to meet overhead, shutting out the sun. There is less than twelve feet between them at the base. Some nineteenth-century travelers, more exalted in imagination than we tend to be now, claimed to have touched both walls at once with outstretched fingers. But this must be set down to the powerful atmosphere of the place: You would need the reach of an extremely well-developed gorilla, and then some.

The awe we feel is chipped away by the throngs of people close before and behind as we proceed along the track. Instructive, and a bit depressing, is the way so many of one's fellow walkers approach what is, after all, a unique experience. They seem consumed with haste. Some spirit of competitiveness comes into play, the inveterate desire to get there first. Those who have come in groups scramble to keep up. Possessed by the wish to overtake, people slither and slide dangerously on the loose stones at the edges of the track. Where the track narrows and there is no space for overtaking, one is aware of audibly breathing presences, close behind, impatient to get past. Remarkably few people seem to pause, slow down, take time to look around them. Yet it is the passing impressions that are the great attraction: the mighty trees, the scalloped rocks, the tumbling stream, the great heights above, slowly hazing as the sun climbs. Almost four hundred species of birds have been recorded here, among them magnificent birds of prey, like the bearded vulture and the golden eagle. There is a chance of catching a glimpse of the Cretan ibex, a splendid kind of wild goat, rare now and protected by the Greek state. The tremendous variety of plant life, orchids, bellflowers, irises, rock plants, and herbs, is found nowhere else. But no; head down, they career onward, only coming to a halt in order to stand in line at one of the infrequent and woefully inadequate public lavatories. The thing is to do the walk, to have done it, to tick it off. Goals and aims and objectives, the culture of achievement, will be the ruin of the human race someday.

Samaria is the most famous of the Cretan gorges— hence the crowds. The numerous others are generally deserted and differ widely in character and constitution. Those who know them have their favorites, rather as is the case with Aegean islands or Roman fountains. For Rackham and Moody, the one best loved is the gorge of Therisso, a ten-mile drive from Chania into the northern fringes of the White Mountains, with its lush vegetation, its shaded, meandering course, and its walls like hanging gardens decked in a variety of endemic plants. For those with a taste for the bare and elemental, there is the gorge that lies behind the Kapsas Monastery in the coastal desert strip on the far southeast of the island, where the average annual rainfall is something like four hundred millimeters. (Compare this with an estimated two thousand millimeters at the highest points in the White Mountains to gain an idea of the range of rainfall from west to east, astonishing on such a small island.) This is a stark and arid landscape, one that the ascetic prophets of old might have felt at home in.

My own favorite is the gorge entered near the village of Zaros in the province of Iraklion. It offers a combination of effects which I think of as essentially Cretan. A little to the west of the village a signed track leads up to the monastery of Agios Nikolaos, a distance of about a mile—on foot from the village it's much less. The entrance to the gorge is higher up, so you can rest in the tranquil, shaded courtyard of the monastery or view the fourteenth-century paintings in the church before setting off for the walk. A climb of half an hour by a steep path brings you to the hermitage of St. Euthymios, a cave with a tiny church built into it and two fine wall paintings still surviving. So you have a monastery, a cave hermitage, and a splendid walk. The gorge of Zaros is short by Cretan standards, perhaps two miles in length, with a good, well-defined path and marvelous views of the Psiloritis mountains continuously before you as you go. This is one of those times on the island—and they are many—when the print of humanity blends in harmony with the unspoiled wildness of the landscape to make an impression quite unforgettable.

However, Crete is rich in alternatives, and if the walk seems too strenuous or the weather too hot, a drive of a few miles west from Zaros, toward Kamares, brings you to another monastery, that of Vrondisi, one of the most beautiful on the island and one of the most important in the history of Cretan monasticism, a center of education and religious art in the period of creative vitality and renewal that took place in the final decades of the Venetian occupation.

The monastery is dedicated to St. Anthony, patron saint of hermits. The outer courtyard, before the main gates, is full of the sound of water falling from the mouths of lion heads sculpted in relief on the fountain, and a plane tree with the dimensions of a cathedral arches over the whole area. It was at Vrondisi that Damaskinos, one of the most important of Cretan religious painters, did some of his best work. Six of the icons he painted here are on permanent display in the gallery of the church of Agia Ekaterini in Iraklion.

On the day of our visit, one of the two remaining monks was sitting in the shade of the fig tree at the entrance, talking gravely to local people. He greeted us with a kind of dignified courtesy. There was no attempt to ask questions or sell us anything, no obtrusive presence making sure that we obeyed the prohibition about taking photographs inside the church, where the rows of frescoed apostles and the Christ of the Last Supper in the apse presented the same grave dignity as they regarded us in the dimness.

Coming back to gorges, that of Samaria has the distinction, together with some smaller ravines that run parallel to it, of giving access, at its southern end, to the sea. So having completed the long, hot walk, emerging at Agia Roumeli, you are presented with the prospect not only of a cold drink but also a refreshing plunge.

This, however, presents you also with a choice as to which first. To reach the shore you have first to pass the bars. We had been distinctly thirsty for quite some time, having foolishly neglected to bring anything to drink with us. Also, the idea of simply sitting down for a while was one that had considerable appeal. The struggle was of the briefest. The bar won hands down. I don't think cold beer has ever tasted so good. By the time we had each had a liter of it, all desire for a refreshing plunge had left us. It was all we could do to make the walk to the boat.

The boats from here go in either direction along the coast. Generally, people take the one going westward to Souyia, thence returning to Chania by road.

But going the other way, to Chora Sfakion, and using it as a base, one can see the mountain villages on the southern side of the White Mountains, the region known as Sfakia.

This is a wild and remote region where roads are few, the climate unrelenting, and the living conditions harsh. The atmosphere of abandonment and desolation one sometimes feels here is in a sense the price the people have paid for their indomitable spirit, their refusal to accept a foreign yoke. This has meant that their villages have been devastated again and again. Through all the centuries of occupation the Sfakians were never completely subdued, resisting Venetian and Turk and German from their mountain fastnesses, and, when for the moment these invaders did not threaten, turning on their own neighbors with equal ferocity. To give one example among many, the people of Zourva were attacked from the rear by the Sfakians in the revolution of 1866, thus saving the Turks from defeat—an attack due entirely to resentment against their fellow countrymen for assuming the leadership of the revolution, a privilege which the Sfakians regarded as exclusively their own. If ever scientists succeed in identifying a warrior gene, it will certainly be found in the people of Sfakia. Their lawless and rapacious spirit is illustrated in the local version of the

Creation. This, as related by Adam Hopkins, begins with an account of the gifts bestowed by God on other parts of the island:

> ... *olives to Ierapetra, Agios Vasilios and Selinou; wine to Malevisi and Kissamou; cherries to Mylopotamos and Amari. But when God got to Sfakia only rocks were left. So the Sfakiots appeared before Him armed to the teeth. "And us, Lord, how are we going to live on these rocks?" And the Almighty, looking at them with sympathy, replied in their own dialect (naturally): "Haven't you got a scrap of brains in your head? Don't you know that the lowlanders are cultivating all these riches for you?"*

It is entirely appropriate that the most splendid of all Cretan heroic legends of resistance against the Turks in the eighteenth and nineteenth centuries should center on the exploits of a Sfakian, Daskaloyiannis, who was born at Anopolis, a village in the foothills behind Chora Sfakion. Also appropriate, since the Sfakians are great singers and storytellers, that he should have found a chronicler from among them. Sixteen years after his death, his story was dictated in a thousand lines of epic verse by an illiterate bard named Pantzelios, a cheesemaker by trade. The scribe was a shepherd. He took down the story slowly and probably painfully—it is hard to believe that he was much accustomed to writing. Here is his description of the process, as translated by Michael Llewellyn Smith who includes an account of the Daskaloyiannis Revolt in his excellent study of the island:

> *I began, and wrote a little every day.*
> *I held the paper and I held the pen*
> *And he told me the story and I wrote it bit by bit.*

To this poem, despite mistakes and heroic exaggerations, we owe most of what is known about the celebrated revolt of Yannis Vlachos, otherwise known as Daskaloyiannis, "John the Teacher," a title of respect rather than a literal description, as in fact he was a ship owner and one of the wealthiest man on the island. It is difficult to imagine anyone less like the Cretan rebel chieftain of tradition. He dressed generally in European clothes, spoke several languages, and had traveled widely in the Mediterranean region. And his political aims went far beyond the usual narrowly territorial uprisings of the Sfakians. He dreamed of freeing Crete and all Greece from the Ottoman occupation and returning her to the comity of Christian nations.

Naturally enough, he turned to the Russians, his co-religionists, for help, and they found in him a useful ally. In fact, from the Russian point of view his appearance was providential. The Russo-Turkish war had just broken out, and it was the job of Count Orloff, Catherine the Great's minister, to foment rebellion against the Turks wherever possible. He found in the enthusiastic and credulous Daskaloyiannis a perfect pawn.

The plans were laid. The Cretan uprising was to coincide with a revolt in the Peloponnese. Orloff undertook to support the rebels from the sea. Armed with this promise, Daskaloyiannis was able to carry the Cretans along with him. The flag of revolt was raised in March 1770. The Sfakian force, probably no more than a thousand men, marched on Chania, the idea being to keep the Turks bottled up inside the walls until the Russian fleet arrived. But the days passed, and no ships were sighted. Without the Russian guns the rebellion was doomed. By May the Turks had entered Sfakia with a force of twenty thousand troops. Heavily outnumbered, the rebels were compelled to retreat to their mountain fastnesses. Still no help came from the Russians.

The Sfakians fought with astonishing bravery and endurance, but by the following spring the situation was desperate, their last lines of defense had been crossed. At this point the pasha of Iraklion wrote to Daskaloyiannis inviting him to give himself up.

> *Trust my letter, whatever they may tell you,*
> *And so leave Sfakia with men to live in her.*
> *When you come and we talk together*
> *All will be settled and we shall be friends.*

With this letter another arrived, this one from Daskaloyiannis's brother, who had already fallen into Turkish hands. In it he urged Daskaloyiannis to accept the pasha's invitation. But he managed to insert into the letter a prearranged code signal indicating that his brother was to take no notice of either letter. In spite of this, Daskaloyiannis decided to surrender. He knew now, after his brother's warning, that he had small chance of saving his life, but he thought he might get better terms for his followers. He made his farewell to wife and children:

> *Come to my arms, children, for me to kiss you,*
> *And be wise until I return again.*
> *Listen to your mother and to your own people—*
> *You have my prayers.*

He gave himself up and was taken to Iraklion. The pasha greeted him with every appearance of friendship, offered him food, wine, coffee, and tobacco, then began a polite interrogation. What was the cause of the revolt? Why didn't you bring your complaints to me?

The cause—you are the cause, you lawless pashas.
That's why I decided to raise Crete in revolt,
to free her from the claws of the Turk.

Hardly the most conciliatory of replies. But then, he hadn't much hope of clemency. And when the pasha, still courteously, asked him for the names of the ring-leaders among the rebels of the Peloponnese, he proudly and angrily refused. You are wasting your breath, he said. Your net has a hole in it, do not hope to catch any fish. This defiance was the end of him. On the pasha's orders, he was taken to the main square of Iraklion and flayed alive. According to the poem he endured this frightful punishment without uttering a sound. But his brother, tied up and obliged to watch the hideous spectacle, could not endure the sight and lost his senses. According to the traditional version of the story, he died mad. The remnants of the Sfakian force, after some years of captivity, returned to the desolation of their ruined villages.

It is difficult to associate the Anopolis of today, the village of the hero's birth, with those desperate and sanguinary days. The thriving village rests quietly in its fertile upland plain, surrounded by fruit trees and fields of wheat. Sfakia as a whole has changed a great deal. The people speak the same language and wear the same style of dress as other Cretans. They are more prosperous now, generally speaking, and more peaceable. They are not always very communicative, but they don't carry weapons anymore—not openly, at least. Communications are better, but the mountains on this part of the south coast plunge abruptly down into the sea, the coastal strip is extremely narrow, hardly more, in many places, than a rocky foreshore. From east to west there are no good roads, and often no roads at all. Those that run north to Chania skirt the White Mountains on either side; there is no way through the heart of the range. And one does not need to wander far from what few roads there are in Sfakia to encounter a landscape that in its bleakness and remoteness recalls the savage past.

CHAPTER FOUR

The MUTABLE FORTRESS

Eastward along the coast from Chania, the main road
keeps close to the shoreline of Souda Bay until it reaches
Kalami, then veers south, turning away from the sea for
a while, joining it again as one approaches Rethymnon.
Near where this change of direction occurs, on a plateau
overlooking the bay, a mile or two inland, lie the ruins
of Aptera, once one of the strongest Greek city-states on
the island. Of very ancient foundation, going back to at
least 1000 B.C., its time of greatest splendor was during
the Hellenistic period, from about 500 B.C. onward.
The city was severely damaged by earthquake early in
the eighth century A.D., and in 823 it was sacked and
more or less completely destroyed by Arab invaders, an

event from which it seems never to have recovered. Excavation—which still continues on the site—has uncovered the remains of massive stone walls, nearly three miles in length, enclosing a wide area, evidence of the importance the city once enjoyed.

After thirteen centuries the evidence of violent events is half buried, grassed over, softened out of recognition, whether it is the violence of natural forces or the savagery of human beings. We had the site to ourselves; in the two hours that we spent there we saw almost no one. We felt a great sense of peace, though we didn't talk about it until later, in this place of ancient battles and dead passions. Perhaps, in my case at least, a kind of acceptance or resignation: All the works of man will in the end be a wide plain, empty of all but stones and flowers, like this one.

Violence and the fear of it are still in evidence, however; it is the single unifying factor in the ruins of this once mighty and prosperous city that has seen so many tenants. All those who came here, having established their power, lived in fear of having that power taken from them and sought in one way or another to guard against attack. The remains of German machine-gun emplacements lie not far from a Turkish fort—or what is left of it—looking out over Souda Bay, and over another fortress lower down with its cannon still in place, and, still lower, over the island fortresses which guard the approaches to this superb natural anchorage, surely one of the finest in the world. Below the German redoubts and the Turkish bastions, Greek naval vessels, guns mounted, pass to and fro.

The city itself was named to commemorate a kind of battle—or so the legend goes. Somewhere among the nearby mountains the Muses challenged the Sirens to a musical contest, and the Sirens lost. In their mortification they stripped off their wings and flung themselves down from the cliffs into the bay, where they were transformed into islands. Another case of Cretan myth stealing: The island of the Sirens, which Odysseus passed on his journey home to Ithaka, is held by everyone else to have been Anthemoessa, off the Italian coast. The Muses, left in the possession of the field, decked themselves in the feathers to celebrate their victory. The literal translation of "Aptera" is "Wingless" or "Featherless," and there was a temple to Artemis in the city, the remains of which are still there, where the goddess was worshiped as Aptera, "Wingless Artemis."

Aptera does not go back so very far as human societies are counted in Crete. When the Dorian Greeks with their iron weapons and warrior cult came down from the north and began to colonize the island, the Bronze Age civilization they replaced had already gone through two thousand years of achievement and decline. But these ruins have everything that can make a Cretan classical site fascinating to visit. Lying on an upland plain, well above sea level, it gives superb views of the high mountains to the south and the great sweep of Souda Bay, with Chania in the distance and the heights of the Akrotiri peninsula jutting out to the north. Recent excavations have revealed, among the tangles of ancient stone and spreading scrub, Doric columns lying where the cataclysm of the earthquake left them, the vestigial walls of a Roman street, the ruins of a Byzantine church, brick-vaulted underground cisterns, dark water still standing in one, and no sound but pigeons' wings.

One can wander at will here, sea on one side, mountain on the other. In spring and early summer the whole area is spread with wildflowers—hollyhock, rockroses, great clusters of dark blue vetch—and alive with the linnets and stonechats and pipits that are the present tenants. For lovers of old stones like us, the wilderness that is left after the fall of ancient cities—which is not like any other kind of wilderness—this place could hardly be better. In those addicted, the attention becomes in a curious way impartial, evenly distributed but without loss of sharpness: The eroded basins of a Roman bathhouse, and the extraordinary vividness of

Aptera: a Roman cistern

the poppies that blaze in the sun among them, have the same interest and the same age.

We searched for traces of fresco painting on the patches of plaster still remaining on the ruinous walls of the Byzantine monastery dedicated to St. John the Theologian. There seemed to be an orangey or ochreous streak here and there, some configuration that might indicate human likeness, human intention. Inveterate, this habit of seeking our own image everywhere. But it is time and decay that have made these marks; they have beauty but no design—or none that we could recognize.

Rethymnon, capital of the province of the same name, is the next town of any size eastward on the road that runs practically the whole length of the island from Kissamou to Sitia, linking all the coastal areas. The principal cities and most of the beach resorts are situated on this north coast.

It's a good road, a lot of it of recent construction, well marked and well surfaced, easily the best road on the island. All the same, we drove warily along it. On Cretan roads the incongruous and unexpected— elements generally present—require a high level of alertness. Someone might be dragging a handcart loaded with oranges, or crossing the road with buckets in a quest for water. Bypass roads are almost nonexistent, and you shift abruptly from the speed and freedom of the open road to a seaside street with shops and bars and parked cars and people in beach dress wandering about, then out again, just as abruptly, with ranks of mountains on one side and the glittering reaches of the Aegean on the other. Also slightly unnerving is the general use of the hard shoulder as a second lane. There should be two lanes, really, on either side, to cope with the volume of traffic, which increases dramatically in the summer. Perhaps the money was lacking for such a large-scale project; the cliffs come down sheer in many places, and there is not much space between them and the shore. However that may be, the hard shoulder, which is narrow when there is one at all, and sometimes strewn with broken stones or the debris of ancient picnics, and which we are conditioned to think of as for emergency use only, is generally regarded by Cretans— who totally lack this conditioning—as an extra lane. Drivers wanting to overtake will sound their horns to make you get over, and they will quickly become angry if you fail to do so.

Cretan driving habits have a quality all their own, which must be seen to be appreciated. It is not self-righteous or unmannerly or neurotically impatient. There is a sort of proud carelessness about it, lordly and dangerous. The quality is best summed up by the Greek word *palikari,* which has no real equivalent in English. The palikari is the hero, the freedom fighter, the patriot. He goes back centuries to the days of Turkish occupation, when he took to the mountains and became an outlaw and fought a guerilla war against the oppressor in which no quarter was shown on either side. You see him in innumerable old pictures, with tasseled cap and fearsome mustachios, breech-loading musket by his side and curving, double-bladed yataghan at his belt.

Village education in Crete hasn't changed so very much since those days. The palikari is a hero still, and a model of behavior, to schoolboy and adult alike. I remember once sitting outside a café in a quiet square when an open sports car of antique design came very fast around the corner and pulled up with extreme suddenness, narrowly missing a war memorial and an ancient woman in black. Out of it stepped a young man who strode into the café without a backward glance. "There goes a palikari," one of the men at a nearby table said, and there was a note of unmistakable admiration in his voice.

The last stretch of road, after it rejoins the coast at the base of the Drapanon peninsula, is spectacular, with the great expanse of the Almirou Bay on your left and the heights of Psiloritis rising before you. The cliffs descend in places very steeply, often to the verge of the road, and where the rock is split or heavily eroded, it shows a warm, reddish color that glows in the sun. On the outskirts of Rethymnon, as on the outskirts of all towns of any size in Crete, there are huge roadside posters advertising cigarettes—a rare sight these days, at least in Western Europe.

Rethymnon is guarded by a Venetian fortress massive in its proportions—it is generally considered the largest the Venetians built anywhere, a response to the increasing frequency of Saracen pirate raids, one by Khair ed-Din Barbarossa in 1538, another by Dragut Rais in 1540, and two by Uluch Ali—an Italian renegade of notable savagery—in 1567 and 1571. The last of these was very destructive; large areas of the town were burned to the ground.

The Venetians succeeded to a large extent in suppressing piracy, but despite the fort's vast size and formidable defenses, Rethymnon fell to the Turks in 1646 after the briefest of sieges. The invaders did not obligingly expose their ships to the Venetian cannon, but attacked from the west and south, bombarding the garrison into submission. Seeing these towering battlements, so costly in men and money and materials, and in the end so unavailing, I was reminded of another empire and another wall, one built by forced labor on the orders of the Roman emperor Hadrian, running from coast to coast across the north of England, constructed to keep out the Picts. The Roman legionaries, used to a warmer climate, must have shivered in those bitter winds, looking always north toward the lands of the accustomed enemy. But the real threat, which no one had envisaged, and against which the wall was useless, came from the south, from the Saxon tribes that would come by sea....

Here in Rethymnon, in the vast open space enclosed by the fortress walls, among the remains of the Venetian barracks and storehouses and cisterns and powder magazines, grow flamboyant red and yellow poppies, and wild oats bleached by the sun, and clumps of white marguerites. Cretan dittany *(Dictamnus creticus)* grows in cracks in the walls. A medicinal infusion of very ancient fame is made from this herb, mentioned by Pliny and Aristotle and Theophrastus, who wrote the first systematic treatise on botany. A plant so celebrated for its healing properties naturally accumulates stories around it. In *The Aeneid* Virgil relates how the hero Aeneas, when suffering from an arrow wound, was healed by means of this wonderful herb, which his mother Aphrodite brought him from Crete. In antiquity, when the Cretan wild goat, or *kri-kri,* was common all over the island, it was believed that they could cure themselves of the arrow wounds inflicted by hunters with a poultice they knew how to make from this plant. This phenomenal sagacity, however, did not prevent the kri-kri from being hunted almost to extinction; today it is found in a wild state only in the gorge of Samaria and the surrounding country.

There is a mosque in the enclosure of the fortress walls, dating from the days of Turkish rule. It was a church before this and a church again after, as Christian and Muslim took their turns in dominating the island. It was the Turks who added the dome, which is beautifully proportioned, and the delicately carved *mihrab* or prayer niche, set in the *qiblah,* the wall that indicates to the faithful the direction of Mecca, to which they turn when they pray. And it was the Turks who organized the interior space into that of a square, a simple enclosure of four walls, in vestigial memory of Mohammed's private house in Medina, where the earliest followers of Islam gathered to pray.

The dome and parts of the windows have been restored in recent years, but this time—finally—not to mark conquest or demonstrate religious supremacy, but because the building is beautiful and can be put to good use. On this particular day we found a busy scene going on inside, with people on ladders, and pieces of plywood cut into various shapes, and all manner of boxes and bundles lying around. A group of artists from Athens were preparing an exhibition of their work. One of them paused to explain it to us. I was relieved that she was able to do this in English. My Greek was once reasonably fluent, good enough at least to argue with taxi drivers or hold my own in discussions about the cost of living and the shortcomings of the Athens government—two principal topics of conversation then and now. But that was half a lifetime ago.

The group was called Touch. They made sculptures, ceramics, mobiles. They had been invited to use this building, which gave them more space than they usually had and so allowed them to show larger and more ambitious works. The woman who was telling me this was clearly exhilarated at the prospect. She was worried about the wind from the sea—they would have to keep the doors closed on that side. But it was a marvelous place for an exhibition. She gestured: the circular space, the clear sea light that came through the windows spaced at intervals all around, the noble proportions of the dome. Very cheering, this enthusiasm, and moving too: Elements that for centuries made this a place of worship for mutually exclusive and hostile faiths now eminently qualify it for devotion of another kind, nondenominational, multiracial, all-inclusive.

This use of former mosques by the Cretans of today is an encouraging sign that the animosities of the past are fading. Crete achieved full independence from Turkish suzerainty only in 1913. When the formal declaration of union with Greece was read out in Chania in November of that year, in the presence of King Constantine and his prime minister, Venizelos, there was a great outburst of public rejoicing. The Greek flag was raised where the Turkish flag had flown, and on the same spot a marble plaque was set up, commemorating the long years of Cretan sufferings at the hands of the invader.

Bitterness takes time to heal. Some years ago I spent a few days on the small island of Simi in the eastern Aegean, one of the group known as the Dodecanese, close to the Turkish coast. I was there to watch the filming of one of my novels—I was curious to see how they would do it, never having witnessed the process before. It is a historical novel, set in the year 1908, at a time when these islands were still under Turkish occupation. In the interests of authenticity it was necessary for the Greek film extras to wear the uniform of Turkish soldiers and for the Turkish flag to be briefly flown and for one or two sentry boxes to be painted red and white, the Turkish colors. These simple requirements caused an immense amount of trouble. The extras needed much persuasion—and probably a higher rate of pay—before they would put on the uniforms. Despite the fact that state permission had been obtained in advance, the local authorities strongly objected to the Turkish colors being shown anywhere on the island, and it took a great deal of diplomacy to soothe their ruffled sensibilities. Almost a century had passed since these islands were united with Greece, but in the minds of those people on Simi it had happened only yesterday.

I didn't mind so very much; in fact, I was more amused than anything else by these squabbles. After all, it wasn't my money. What bothered me rather more was that no one but the director seemed to have read the novel, and production assistants kept asking me who I was and what I was doing there. I did, however, though very briefly, experience a surge of authorial power on Simi, something that happens rarely. On the island of my novel there were little horse-drawn traps waiting at the quay side to take foreign visitors to the hotel. But the snag about this was that on Simi there were no horses. No point in horses on a rocky little island like that. So horses had to be brought by ship from the mainland. When I saw those horses standing in a line, harnessed to their carriages, I must confess to a feeling that approached omnipotence. All that trouble and expense just for a few lines, less than a paragraph ...

On this day of our visit to Rethymnon, in the Nerandzes Mosque in the Old Town, a concert of classical music is in progress. By contrast there is the Karen Pasha mosque near Platia Iroon, its courtyard weedy and littered, its gates barred, its domes and arches crumbling

The Karen Pasha mosque

and ruinous, without even a name anywhere now to identify it for the passerby. Standing out, with some Ottoman echo of Cretan indestructibility, a beautiful Muslim gravestone with a design of foliage and flowers.

Rethymnon is a great town to wander about and get lost in, a fascinating promiscuous jumble of architectural styles, Venetian and Ottoman and Greek coexisting side by side, carved wooden balconies and stair rails, bricked-in arches, stone fountains tucked away in odd corners, arabesques over a gateway, the Corinthian capitals of some neoclassical mansion converted to multiple occupation. Clues to the past and the present, a lesson in architecture and history at one and the same time.

Sooner or later, to restore your sense of direction, you will emerge to a sight of the sea again, a glinting, slightly ruffled cobalt expanse on this summer day, capable of all manner of violence, notoriously treacherous, the source of all the doubtful benefits and certain troubles that have gone to make up the island's history from remotest times.

CHAPTER FIVE

WITHIN

the LABYRINTH

Eastward again to Iraklion, official capital of Crete since 1971. After the attractive harbor towns of Chania and Rethymnon, which are easy to explore on foot and still retain vestiges of a traditional way of life, most of Iraklion is sprawling and featureless. The city suffered extensive damage from bombing raids during the Second World War, and the postwar reconstruction was carried out in haste, without much planning and without much care for style.

Despite its present prosperity—this is the wealthiest region of the island—Iraklion has an unmistakable look of lost function, of a city somehow sidetracked, traduced by history. This is a sad condition and one

Iraklion: the Venetian fortress

difficult to demonstrate by example, but it is summed up by the vast Venetian harbor and the great fort that guards its entrance. A fleet of Venetian war galleys could have anchored here once, under those protecting cannon. Walls and fortifications are still in place. But the harbor cannot accommodate modern vessels. Even the ferryboats plying to the mainland—the main traffic by sea—have to dock at the massive, and massively ugly, concrete wharves nearby. The arsenals and shipyards the Venetians built are lost in a sea of traffic.

The city's history, and that of Crete as a whole, is written in its successive names. The original village was named after Herakles, the mythical Greek hero and strongman. In the ninth century the invading Arabs built a fortified town here, which they called Khandak, the Arabic word for the kind of large moat that formed part of the town's defenses. This became Chandrax for the Byzantines, who expelled the Arabs in 961, and Candia for the Venetians, who took over the island in 1204. The original name was not restored until early in the twentieth century, after the last of the Turkish occupying troops had been sent packing. It was as Candia that the city enjoyed its greatest power and prestige becoming one of the great cities of Europe, an important trading post and outfitting center for the Crusades. And it was virtually impregnable. Whatever the shortcomings of the Venetians, they knew how to build forts: Even when the Turks controlled the rest of the island, they took another twenty-one years to conquer this last bulwark of Christianity in the eastern Mediterranean—probably the longest sustained siege of any city in recorded history.

We lost some time on an unsuccessful quest for a reasonably good bookshop. It seems somehow significant, somehow typical, that a city this size, with something like 100,000 inhabitants, capital of the island, didn't have one. Crete does not abound in them anyway, but there are better ones at both Chania and Rethymnon.

Put out by this failure, I tried gloomily to remember when, if ever, I saw a Cretan reading a book. I was brought to regret these unkind thoughts when the bookshop where I had asked for a book obtained it for me in three days and phoned to tell me it had arrived.

The Church of St. Titus, at 25 Avgoustou Street, near Kalergon Square, sums up in its architectural history the ebb and flow of power on the island. Titus was a disciple of St. Paul the Apostle, who appointed him first bishop of Crete. His church in Iraklion was founded by the Byzantines, taken over and rebuilt by the Venetians, turned into a mosque by the Turks, restored by them after the earthquake of 1856, renovated by the Orthodox Church after the Turks had departed, reconsecrated in 1925.

Quite a checkered career. But through all these vicissitudes, we discovered one object that has survived in its pristine state, and that is Titus's skull, which has been preserved as an object of devotion—the rest of his body was never recovered. True, the skull has traveled about a good deal. Until the early Middle Ages it was kept in the ancient basilica at Gortyn, also dedicated to the saint; then it was moved to Iraklion; then—out of fear of the invading Turks—transferred to Venice and kept there for some centuries. Finally, in 1966, it was restored to the capital and reposes in a

Iraklion: The Church of St. Titus

reliquary in this quiet church, free from further threats and alarms, or so one hopes.

We found other things too that have escaped mutilation. The Christians pulled down the minaret and surmounted the dome with a cross, but in the small courtyard in front of the church the unpretentious Ottoman fountain still keeps its place, with its exquisitely carved stone, its channel for the washing of feet, and outlets for running water—always running water for the Muslim lustration. The fountain is beautiful, and it has survived by virtue of its modest dimensions—there is a lot to be said for keeping low to the ground.

The churches of Crete can be a guide to the labyrinth of history even when they have long ceased to be buildings at all. The Monastery of San Francesco exists no longer, but it was once the most imposing Catholic foundation on the island, built by the Venetians in the first century of their rule. Now Iraklion's Archaeological Museum covers the site. But it has not vanished altogether. While it was still being used as a mosque, the severe earthquake of 1856 brought most of it down, but Turkish troops rescued the door frame and built it into their barracks, for reasons not clear, perhaps in the hope of Allah's blessing, though it was a Christian door frame originally, having been donated to the church in 1410 by Pope Alexander V, a Cretan named Petros Philargos, who, according to some sources, had previously been a monk at the monastery. There were no less than three popes at that time and considerable doubt as to who was St. Peter's legitimate heir. Alexander died after only ten months in office, a mysterious death—many believed he had been poisoned by his successor. The barracks crumbled away in their turn, but the door survived: It now serves as northern entrance to the law court on Dikeossinis Street and must have witnessed the passage of a good many malefactors. Five hundred years and a mystery or two, all in the span of a door frame.

The Church of Agia Ekaterini on the square of the same name, which we arrived at going westward down Kalokerinou toward the Chania Gate, has been put to a use which—like the former mosque inside the fortress walls in Rethymnon and the former Church of San Francesco in Chania, now a museum—makes very good sense indeed. Formally a celebrated monastic academy and art school, it is now a museum of religious art, housing a collection of Cretan icons it would be difficult to match elsewhere, in particular several by Michalis Damaskinos, a contemporary of El Greco, also Cretan, less famous than him but a very considerable artist, one of the first Cretan painters to introduce elements of

Renaissance humanism into the severely formal tradition of Byzantine icon and fresco painting.

Agia Pelagia, a few miles west of Iraklion, is where a lot of people choose to stay who want to combine a beach holiday with trips to Knossos and various other Minoan sites in the vicinity of the city. The phrase "a lot of people" seems like an understatement in view of the multitudes that descend on the region at the onset of summer. The headland above the village is more or less entirely staked out by huge hotel complexes, places where you can easily get lost—it might take you a quarter of an hour to walk through the beautiful gardens from your chalet or villa or bungalow to the nearest place where you can get a cup of coffee, or find someone to tell you where a cup of coffee is to be got.

This is the exclusive, expensive face of tourism in Crete. The other face can be found below, in the continuous string of bars, discos, tavernas that front the narrow strip of beach and extend inland to a wilderness of car-rental agencies, fast-food eating places, supermarkets, and a jumble of apartment houses and small hotels and half-finished building projects. The roads designed to link these places haven't had time yet to catch up. They too are often half finished, sometimes hardly started, sometimes ending in piles of rubble or vacant lots. The pace of development outstrips the maps, however up-to-date these may appear to be. What looks blessedly empty on the map turns out to be in full spate of building. There is a point, not easily measurable but nonetheless real, when the influx of visitors and the changes of structure needed to accommodate them passes from sustainable to destructive. And it is a point of no return. The anthropologist Sonia Greger, writing in 1993, already sounded a warning note:

> *Tourism along the north-east coastal strip of Crete has, I would say, reached crisis stage with respect to the near break-down of traditional values, hospitality and sense of community…. One cause of crisis in tourist development is escalating competition between locals, as they throw out their traditional means of support and subsistence.*

The larger, more expensive hotels overlooking the bay also cause damage to local communities, in this case by virtually depriving them of their own land. Extensive areas of the promontory, including large stretches of the shoreline, are closed off. By Greek law everyone has the right of access to the shore, regarded as common land. This is an excellent principle, but it is not applied in practice. The hotels have imposing gates and entrance driveways, and security guards to keep an eye on who comes and goes. Unless you are a guest or very good at bluffing, you are unlikely to get through. This means that a local inhabitant who once swam from these beaches, or kept a small boat for fishing, or walked on the cliffs and enjoyed the splendid views across the bay, and who was accustomed to regard these things as his birthright, has been—as the result of a stroke of the pen in some remote office—entirely dispossessed.

Such vast hotels are in any case founded on a wrong concept of what a hotel should be. "Megalux" is the effect aimed at. The "mega" is present in the hundreds of detached bungalows, in the acres of gardens, the vast, marble-appointed reception areas. But the "lux" part is lacking. The capital outlay has been enormous, the need to recoup very urgent. Package tours are the quick way to do this. For these hotels the ideal visitor is not a private person but a unit, a number, part of a package. A spirit of suspicion prevails. The guest must furnish himself with a card that has his category on it; without this he is lost, unable to reply satisfactorily to the hotel staff who are constantly asking him who and what he is. In one hotel with a five-star deluxe rating, one of the most expensive on the island, outside a breakfast room with seating for a thousand people, so large that one can hardly see across it, there is a notice in various languages requesting the guests not to walk away with the knives and spoons. The women who work as cleaners are routinely searched at the gatehouse before being allowed to leave.

At the entrance to the dining room an impeccably dinner-jacketed headwaiter, having glanced at our card, murmured that in our case meals were extra. We found out that—just as in the case of people who want to avoid being mugged on the street—you must look as if you know where you are going. As we wandered bemused among clumps of tamarisk and orange groves and volleyball pitches and Olympic-size pools and pala-, tial conference rooms, a security guard in the dress of a Cretan bandit, festooned with weapons, emerged from the shrubbery and asked to see the card proving we were bona fide guests.

Lying just a few miles south of Iraklion, the magnet that draws so many people to this region of Crete is Knossos, indisputably one of the greatest prehistoric sites in the world. This is where the labyrinth, which has exercised the Western imagination for millennia, is said to have been, though its real nature is still disputed. Some maintain that it derives from the Minoan habit of agglutinative building, adding rooms to already existing rooms till their houses and palaces came to resemble mazes—in that case, perhaps the palace of Knossos, which in its heyday had more than a thousand rooms on five floors, was itself the labyrinth.

Others argue that the name derives from religious practice. *Labrys* in Lydian means "doubled-headed ax," which was an object of cult worship among the Minoans. So *labyrinthos* might mean "the place of the sacred ax." Costis Davaras mentions the belief held by some that the real place of the labyrinth was not Knossos at all, but the cave at Skotino, some miles east of Iraklion. As already noted, it is difficult to pursue any line of inquiry regarding Crete, or take any route, without coming across a cave before long. This is one of the most impressive on the island, 530 feet deep, with a main chamber like the nave of a cathedral and winding galleries.

The theory I like most but believe least is that the labyrinth refers to Cretan dancing patterns. At the close of Book Eighteen of *The Iliad,* Homer describes a Cretan folk dance whose weaving motions make maze-like patterns that form and dissolve. Here it is in Robert Fitzgerald's translation:

> *A dancing floor as well,*
> *he fashioned, like that one in royal Knossos*
> *Daedalus made for the Princess Ariadne …*
> *Trained and adept they circled there with ease*
> *The way a potter sitting at his wheel*

Will give it a practised whirl between his palms
To see it run; or else, again, in lines
As though in ranks, they moved on one another:
Magical dancing!

Independently of the theories, the ancient myths
have remained. The palace of Knossos was the heart of
Bronze Age Crete; at the heart of the palace was the
labyrinth; and at the heart of the labyrinth was the monstrous Minotaur. Here the hero Theseus came, here the
king's daughter Ariadne fell in love with him and gave
him the ball of twine which helped him to find his way
out after slaying the monster, here Daedalus the master
artificer made the wings for himself and his son Ikarus
so that they could escape from the maze. Ikarus, it will
be remembered, flew so near the sun, the wax that
bound his feathers melted and he plunged into the sea.
The island in the Sporades where his body was washed
up is named after him, Ikaria. A real island, a mythic
punishment for human rashness …

The excavation of Knossos by the great British
archaeologist Arthur Evans has itself by now passed into
the zone of myth—at least, it has assumed that blend of
fact and legend somehow characteristically Cretan.
What led him to it seems to have been an accident of his
own physical constitution more than anything else. Joan

Evans, in her biography of him, tells us that he was extremely shortsighted. If he held things very close to his eyes he could see them in the most amazing detail, but at any farther distance everything was blurred. Not much of a blessing in general terms, but it enabled Evans to make out with phenomenal exactitude the hieroglyphics on the bead seals—an earlier form of signet ring—that he came across in various parts of the eastern Mediterranean. The Athenian dealers told him that most of these came from Crete. And it was in fact in Crete that he found them again. He could not decipher the signs, but he recognized affinities with Egyptian and Mesopotamian hieroglyphics. They brought him to the conviction, one which changed the whole course of his life, that on this island there had once existed a highly developed civilization, the remains of which still lay under the ground.

It is not given to many men, proceeding almost single-handed, acting on a solitary conviction and guided by a mixture of deduction and intuition, to demonstrate to the world the existence of a hitherto totally unsuspected civilization. It was given to Evans.

In March 1899 he recruited Cretan workmen and began digging into the mound of Kephala at Knossos. He was at first looking for further examples of the hieroglyphics he had found on the seal stones. He was never to succeed in deciphering these, but in a matter of days he realized that much more than hieroglyphics was involved in the enterprise. He was in the process of uncovering the remains of a palace complex vast in its extent, showing evidence of engineering and architectural techniques so advanced that they could only have belonged to a highly developed society. It was still commonly believed at the time that European civilization began with the Greeks, somewhere about the year 700 B.C. Evens realized he was being given the opportunity to supply a gap of 1,500 years in Europe's knowledge of its own past.

Amazing things were unearthed at Knossos in these last months of the nineteenth century. An early find was a cup-bearer fresco, discovered in two pieces, the first representation ever brought to light of a young man of the prehistoric Cretan Bronze Age, the society that Evans was to call Minoan. Day by day the ground plan of the palace was uncovered: porticos, bathhouses, courtyards, stairways, the throne room with the throne of King Minos still in its original place. But perhaps the most remarkable find of all was the remains of a fresco showing a young man somersaulting, with incredible hardihood and acrobatic skill, over the back of a charging bull, and a girl standing with arms outstretched as if to catch him as he lands. In the months that followed they encountered this theme of bull vaulting again and again. The meaning still eludes us—at least it is still argued about, which comes to the same thing. Popular sport? Gladiatorial contest? Religious practice based on the worship of the bull? Or are the stories of human sacrifice true after all? Was one of these bull leapers the hero Theseus, as we find related in Mary Renault's novel *The Bull from the Sea?*

Visiting Knossos by car these days confronts one with a different kind of puzzle—and yet another example of Cretan enterprise. Which is the official parking lot? On the last half mile or so of the road that leads to the site, we counted seven at least, competing for custom. The official one was free, the others were not, though they all had large and prominent and closely similar signs proclaiming their identity as the true Knossos CarPark. Only later, when we had been maneuvered into one of the cramped and rutted unofficial parks and paid for our ticket, did we both, simultaneously, realize the difference: The official parking lot was the one with the least conspicuous sign, and it had no person at the roadside in an official-looking cap waving and smiling and guiding you in.

To our dismay the site itself was swarming with visitors, many in large groups brought by tour buses, conducted by cheerfully positive guides who give out as established fact what must surely, after so long and on such sketchy evidence, be matters of speculation. "This was the queen's bedchamber, and this was her dressing room, where the ladies-in-waiting attended on her...."

We clamber to identify the rooms, understand the layout of this vast place, more like a town than a single building, where monarchs and priests and artisans and slaves lived nearly four thousand years ago. A longish line of people are waiting for their turn to view the throne room, one of the most celebrated sights of Knossos. After ten minutes or so of gradual forward movement we reach the cagelike bars which, separate the anteroom from the throne room. We peer through the bars, straining to make out details in the dim interior: the pale, streaky-looking gypsum throne of Minos on the right, still standing on the spot where it was found, flanked by copies of the original frescoes of crouching griffins; the sunken bath, perhaps for ritual cleansing—Minos, it seems, was both priest and king; a sort of recess beyond, perhaps serving as a shrine, or perhaps ... But now there sounds the voice of the latter-day priestess, guardian of the sacred precinct, who is keeping an eye on things from her bench in the anteroom: "Move along, please! Don't stay too long at the viewing point!"

We have been allowed approximately thirty seconds. Shuffling forward again, we get trapped in a corner,

Knossos: the queen's apartments

surrounded by seemingly enormous Scandinavians, in our ears the loud and confident voices of various guides. Not panic, perhaps, but feelings of oppression certainly. We are in a modern version of the Knossos labyrinth, how can we get out? Here, as in a different way in those vast beach hotels that specialize in packages, being the solitary individual has its snags. Wandering about the ruins, trying to make head and tail of things, the single person gets hemmed in, confused by alien voices. The member of the group does not suffer this fate: He has the comfort of numbers, he occupies the space, he is with the others, listening to the same voice, looking at the same things.

Very difficult, in such a crowd, to exercise the powers of imagination and intuition needed to feel the wonder of this place, get a sense of the remote society that once flourished here. We all get in one another's way with our exclamations, our sun hats, our ungainly scramblings. Only at certain times, early in the morning, or during the hot middle hours of the day when the bus excursions have their scheduled lunchtime, the extraordinary nature of the place comes over one in a wave. The storerooms with their great earthenware jars for oil and grain; the workshops where the jewelers and smiths and potters made the objects for use and decoration never since surpassed for the quality of their workmanship and design;

the royal quarters with their spacious, light-filled apartments; the vivid frescoes depicting people in their daily lives and all manner of birds and animals and flowers—dolphins, partridges, octopuses, lilies. Any of these things, even the smallest detail, can become a focal point for wonder, and one begins to understand what Pendlebury, who knew more about the palace of Minos than just about anyone else, meant when he wrote thus of its final destruction, probably due to a combination of earthquake, volcanic eruption on the nearby island of Santorini, and the onslaught of invaders: "With that wild spring day at the beginning of the fourteenth century B.C. something went out of the world which the world will never see again; something grotesque perhaps, something fantastic and cruel, but also something very lovely."

One thing which makes Knossos different from all other Minoan sites on Crete is the reconstructions that were carried out by Sir Arthur Evans—as he by then had become—mainly in the course of the 1920s. In his passion for what he had discovered, his desire to protect the recently exposed remains from the weather, his wish to make the layout of the palace more easily understood by the visitor, he used the architectural details he found in fresco fragments to reconstruct some of the buildings, making use of bricks, metal girders, and cement to

Knossos: Shield frescoes from the head of the grand staircase

rebuild the columns and door lintels destroyed in those distant fires.

This use of modern materials caused heated arguments at a time when there was a strongly romantic feeling about ancient remains. Evans was called the "builder of ruins" in the French press. Many people since then have felt that he went too far, that his use of the frescoes was too subjective. But there can be no doubt that he saved some important buildings from collapse, among them the grand staircase of the palace, regarded as unique in architectural history, with five flights of stairs still preserved in situ.

Unreconstructed, altogether less adorned and distinctly less crowded, are the palace of Festos, second largest of the Minoan palaces, overlooking the bay of Mesaras on the south coast, and the smaller palace of Agia Triada two miles nearer the coast. These are sites rich in archaeological interest with superb views over the plain of Mesara to the Libyan Sea. I am not by nature very exacting when it comes to exploring ancient remains. It doesn't really give me any great satisfaction to know whether this niche or that was actually the family shrine, or precisely how high the staircase was, or—in any detail—how the water pipes were all joined up. I would only forget these things again. Making precise identifications on these Minoan sites is a headache anyway, for clues are scanty, and on-site information even scantier. Wandering here on a summer morning with the evidence of ancient life all around one, the olive groves and vineyards covering the plain below, the majestic peaks of Psiloritis rising to the north and the warm breath of Africa against your face—it is difficult to imagine a pleasanter way of spending an hour or two.

In 1908, inside a small chamber at Festos, one of the most famous finds in the history of Minoan excavation was made, the disk of baked clay, later to be known as the Festos Disk, dating from around 1700 B.C. Its provenance is still disputed, but the evidence indicates that it was made in Crete. At present housed in the Archaeological Museum of Iraklion, it is something truly to marvel at, a solid disk roughly six inches in diameter, completely covered back and front with ideographs inscribed in spiral form from the circumference to the center, 241 signs in all, among them running figures, heads crowned with feathers, ships, shields, birds and beasts and insects, each one impressed with great care on the wet clay using some kind of stamp. And all this several thousand years before Gutenberg!

Despite a century of efforts to decipher the script, no agreement has yet been reached. Various theories have been advanced. Was it a hymn to the Lord of the Rain, a set of building instructions, a list of provisions for the army, an anthem to a pantheon of gods? Some pretty unlikely solutions have been offered. At different times, linguists have sought to demonstrate that the text derives from Basque, or Finnish, or Magyar.

The road back to Iraklion branches northward at Agii Deka, and soon afterward runs past the ruins of ancient Gortyn, which was a Minoan city but saw its greatest power and importance in the classical period, first under the Greeks and then under the Romans. Three momentous landings outline the story of the city, the first of them—naturally, since this is Crete— mythological. Zeus, having fallen in love with Europa, a daughter of Agenor, king of Tyre in Phoenicia, assumed the form of a beautiful white bull. He seemed so gentle, the girl was enchanted by him and was eventually persuaded to climb on his back. Before she knew what was happening, she was riding out to sea, on the way to Crete. He brought her to Gortyn, where they became lovers. One of their three sons was Minos, whose throne room we got a thirty-second view of at Knossos. Crete then, not only gave Europe its name, it was where Europe began, a truth Cretans have always known.

The second landing occurred in the first century A.D., that of Titus, the disciple of St. Paul, who appointed him first bishop of Crete and gave him the task of overseeing the early Christian church on the island. "For this cause I left thee in Crete," the Apostle says in his Epistle to Titus, "that thou shouldst set in order the things that are wanting." Paul's opinion of the Cretans, as we have seen, was not very high. Titus was martyred at Gortyn, and the ruins of the sixth-century basilica of the cross-in-square type that was built on the site of his martyrdom are among the most impressive to be seen here, with three apses and a section of the vaulting still standing. Under the Romans Gortyn became capital of the province of Crete and Libya, with a population of a quarter million, and it continued in wealth and importance under the Byzantines, who took over the island in A.D. 330.

The third landing—and the last—was that of the Saracens in A.D. 825. In accordance with their general policy throughout the island, they visited the city with fire and sword, and it was never rebuilt.

Legendary beginnings, a period of glory, total devastation—it is a familiar paradigm in the history of Crete. There is an abiding desolation in the remains of Gortyn that I have not felt elsewhere among the ruined cities of Crete, probably due to the huge area over which the ruins are spread. They extend on either side of the road, acre after acre of them, through thickets of bramble and choked ditches and plowed fields and olive groves. The local people have used the marble of temples and the granite of churches to repair their walls. Gortyn, especially on the south side of the road in the area bordering the River Mitropolitanos, provides a striking example of a universal process: the reversion of buildings to ruins and ruins to rubble and rubble to dust. This feeling gives a melancholy to the place and seems to rub away the distinctions of time and period: The ruins of the Roman governor's palace, or of the Greek temple to Pythian Apollo, seem no older than the broken walls of an abandoned sheep pen. It is the same with people: The dead belong to one state and one period only.

To rescue one from melancholy, there is always the vitality and warmth of the people and the unfailing charm of the landscape, which can turn the accidental or unplanned into memorable experience. The region northwest of Gortyn is spectacularly beautiful. One day, in an attempt to go on foot from the village of Vorizia to the Valsamonero Monastery, we took a wrong turn. We realized our mistake after a while, but continued along the track we were on, impelled by the wildness and purity of the light among these hills—like the first light of the world—and by the play of shadow on the mountain peaks to the north, still capped with snow. The olive trees were in flower and the air was full of birdsong. Incredibly ancient, these olives, the trunks twisted and gnarled into tormented shapes. Seeing them, it is easy to understand the pervasive stories of metamorphosis found in Greek myths and in the Latin poets who inherited them. Poems of escape from death or ravishment, last-minute rescues by some suddenly compassionate god, plants struggling to turn into humans, humans striving to find escape in plants.

The olive was already cultivated on this island two thousand years before Christ. It is easy to believe, seeing these time-wrenched shapes, that some of the present trees go back that far. They don't, of course, not quite, but one of the oldest olive trees in Europe is on Crete, at

Loutro in Sfakia, with annual rings that date to well over two thousand years ago. Any olive with a diameter of seven feet or so will go back to the Middle Ages.

The path climbed up into the hills and there were ravens nesting in the crags above us and a kestrel circling below and, above the olives, great spreads of the splendid Greek fir, which you rarely see at altitudes of less than two thousand feet. This tree is dedicated to Pan, god of shepherds. He and Vorias (the North Wind) were both in love with a nymph called Pitys. She chose Pan as being less blustering and turbulent. In revenge Vorias blew her off a cliff. Pan found her dying and transformed her into his sacred tree, the fir, which was called Pitys in memory of her. Since then she cries every time the north wind blows, and her tears are the drops of resin that drip from her cones in autumn.

We tramped for a good many miles that day and were given a handful of oranges when we came to lower ground by gravely courteous people who quite clearly thought we were out of our minds to be clambering about when there was no need. I thanked them in Greek, which may at least have served to reassure them that we were not from some altogether different planet. Dusk fell, there was no time, we didn't see the Valsamonero Monastery, with its fifteenth-century frescoes, painted by Konstantinos Rikos and said to be among the finest in Crete. But the monastery gave us a great trip and one can't ask more than that. As the Alexandrian Greek poet Kavafis says in his poem about Ithaka, the kingdom of Odysseus, who found his way back there from Troy after many adventures, it's no use asking anything from the island when you finally arrive: It has already made you the supreme gift of the journey.

There is one monument at Gortyn which has endured in much the same way that the olive trees have, strongly rooted like them. When the Odeon, or Covered Theater, was built here about A.D. 100, in the time of the Emperor Trajan, a much older wall was incorporated, as it had been incorporated in a succession of earlier buildings—a wall inscribed in Dorian Greek with a code of laws dating from the fifth century B.C. Over six hundred lines in length, the script reads one line from left to right, the next from right to left, so that the eye can follow the text continuously. It is the first codified system of laws known to Europe and one of the most amazing documents in existence anywhere.

Not that it illustrates the principle of equality before the law, so dear to us today, and even today more common in the breach than the observance. These are the laws of a society that was still tribal, still governed by rigid distinctions of caste. For rape committed against a free person the fine was 1,200 obols, while for the rape of a household slave the fine went from one to 24 obols, "depending on circumstances." What strikes us today is not the particular notion of justice contained in the statutes, but the reverence with which they have been treated over such a great span of time, the beauty of the lettering, the continuous incorporation into new buildings as the old ones crumbled away. An early example, however unequal the laws, of that striving for order, for shelter from violence and chaos common to every human society. The form of the Odeon can still be made out: the semicircle of the amphitheater, some remains of benches, but most of it now is little more than broken stones. The Gortyn Code, however, is still intact, an abiding monument to the principle of legality. It is housed now in its own brick shelter, protected from the weather. Protected from people too—you can only look at it from a distance, through bars.

Having seen where the people we call Minoans lived, and formed some idea of their surroundings and the circumstances of their lives, the natural progression is to go on to see the things they made. Whatever reservations one has about the attractiveness of modern Iraklion, the city's archaeological museum is one of the finest to be found anywhere, and its collection of Minoan artifacts quite unique. Here, beautifully displayed in room after room, are the objects that give physical expression to the spirit of that remote society, and trace the way that spirit developed and changed, from its beginnings in the Neolithic period ten thousand years ago to the high culture of the Palace period, between 2000 and 1450 B.C., and on to the time of invasion from the mainland and subsequent decline.

Among a huge variety of objects from all over Minoan Crete—Knossos, Malia, Festos, Tylissos, Zacros, Agia Triada, Gournia—are some that through the fame and mystery that surrounds them have become semi-legendary. Here is the Festos Disk, already mentioned, exquisite and baffling, printed on fresh clay three and a half thousand years ago, making it the first ever printed document. Here is the sarcophagus found in a tomb in the precincts of the palace at Agia Triada, its surface completely covered with painted plaster, depicting scenes of ritual worship and the cult of the dead. Once again we are in the toils of speculation. The jar the priestess is emptying, does it contain blood? What is the significance of the black bird that sits between two double axes, or the model ship that one man is holding out to another? Such things remind us that for all the patience we can muster and all the resources for research at our disposal, there is a world of values and beliefs forever beyond the reach of our understanding.

Then there is the celebrated ivory figurine of the bull leaper, caught in the very moment he is vaulting the bull's foreparts, about to perform the astounding somersault which will land him on his feet again on the other side of the animal. The musculature and anatomical form of the body are rendered with what seems absolute fidelity until one sees that the arms and legs are longer than they should be—a device we meet with in contemporary art, revolutionary then, designed to convey the grace of the movement without loss of tension. His hair is made separately, of bronze threads. Priest, gladiator, devotee, slave, star athlete, what was he?

From the same period and the same place—the palace at Knossos—are two faience figures of snake goddesses, one slightly taller than the other so perhaps mother and daughter, both with prominent, naked breasts and elaborate skirts and coiled snakes wreathed around arms and body—the smaller also holds up rampant snakes, one in each hand. The snake was a principal object of worship among the Minoans, for whom it represented eternity, immortality, and reincarnation. The goddesses were fashioned for small household shrines and worshiped as domestic divinities, guardians of the house.

For many, the crowning glory of the museum is the room containing the Kamares ware dating back to the Old Palace period. This beautiful pottery owes its name to the Kamares cave in the eastern zone of Psiloritis, where a great quantity of it was discovered. A group of Italian archaeologists, in the 1890s, exploring caves in this wild and rugged terrain, stumbled upon a treasure trove of painted pottery, some fragmented, some virtually whole, bowls, cups, jugs, amphora, all of unique quality. This came at a time when almost nothing was known about the Minoans. They had not even been named yet, the work of excavation at Knossos had not yet properly begun. I have never read an account of this discovery, but I like to imagine that the magnitude of it came to them only gradually and with growing delight as they moved here and there in the recesses of the cavern, the light from their lamps falling on these heaps of pots, which had rested so long unseen and unappreciated, retaining their glowing colors in the dark of the cave.

Now we know what they at the time didn't, that most of this pottery was fashioned in the palace work-shops of Knossos and Festos. They superbly illustrate the Minoan feeling for dynamic movement based on interweaving patterns. The tentacles of an octopus, the shoots and tendrils of a plant, the fronds of a palm tree mingle with abstract curvilinear designs, spiral and coil and turn in on themselves, in a way that recalls yet again the stories of the labyrinth, that seemingly endless elaboration and extension of rooms in the palaces. Perhaps the maze, as idea and as design, was a fundamental element of Minoan sensibility.

So we wandered from room to room in this splendid museum, tracing the development of a culture, a search for form, which is a search also for meaning, through all the meanderings of taste and fashion. A strong religious feeling is expressed here, and a joy in natural forms and in the pleasures of the senses. There is no depiction of war. The Minoan people, throughout most of their history, enjoyed that sort of freedom from predators that allows animals or insects to flourish in certain habitats. The only way to attack Crete was by sea, and for that a strong navy was needed, but no one in the Mediterranean world of that time seems to have possessed such a navy—except the Cretans themselves. The Minoan kingdom was a thalassocracy, a sovereignty of the sea. They traded far and wide, they established colonies, they cleared the sea routes of pirates, but they fought no battles on their own soil, until the final ones that put an end to them.

It was a combination of circumstances that brought them down. Between 1500 and 1450 B.C. Crete suffered a succession of earthquakes which damaged the centers of power, weakening the island so that it became vulnerable to invasion just at the time when the power of

Mycenae on the Greek mainland was expanding. The Mycenaeans were the first to occupy the island. When their day was over, it was the turn of Greek tribes from the north, with their sky god and their iron weapons. More primitive than those they conquered, they were unable to absorb or adapt what they found, or put anything in place of what they destroyed. It was the beginning of a dark age in the eastern Mediterranean that was to last for some centuries. The palaces were never rebuilt and never again inhabited, the invaders regarding them as uncanny, haunted places. Writing disappeared completely; what art was produced was crude and botched.

In the objects on display in the last rooms on the ground floor one feels this crushing of the spirit as an almost palpable presence, like an affliction, as if the collective mind of this gifted people had been stricken by the equivalent in cultural terms of Alzheimer's disease. There is an increasing number of large, crudely molded terra-cotta figures of goddesses with rounded lumps for breasts and blind, coarsened faces. Their arms are raised in the conventional posture of prayer. Stand away a little and look at these groups, and they seem like creatures in mourning for their own ruin and for their ruined world, raising their arms in terrible mute grief.

On the floor above, however, lightness returns to the spirit. Here are the rooms devoted to Minoan wall paintings. Their qualities of gaiety and elegance and exuberant color are undeniable. More doubtful is the accuracy with which some of them have been reconstituted from the fragments of fresco, sometimes very scanty, that remained. Much dedicated scholarship has gone to reassembling these fragments, but also a considerable amount of dubious ingenuity and wishful thinking. Perhaps the most famous example of this, and among the most famous of all Minoan frescoes, is the "Prince with Lilies," as he still continues, in spite of everything, to be called. Wasp-waisted, naked but for a loincloth, he wears a garland of lilies and a plumed crown, and he walks among flowers, holding an animal thought to be a griffin on a leash. Arthur Evans himself privately considered the fragments from which the prince was assembled to be quite unconnected, the head belonging to a king or god, the torso to an athlete of some kind, the rest of the body to someone else altogether. But who would be content with a barrowload of painted plaster chips when he could make a prince out of it? Evans succumbed, as sometimes before, to the desire to add luster to the world he had uncovered. The restorers, perhaps wanting to please him, on their own initiative painted over some parts to give an impression of unity to the assemblage.

The prince remained unquestioned for half a century, until 1960, when it was discovered, quite by accident, that the animal on the leash was not a griffin but a sphinx, and furthermore that it was the sphinx who should be wearing the plumed diadem, not the man at all. When faith is once disturbed, queries multiply. It began to be pointed out that the neck was joined to the torso at an extremely odd angle, that in terms of human anatomy the pose was impossible, that he could not be leading any kind of animal, whether legendary or real. More recently he has been declared to be not a prince at all but the god of eternal youth, flanked by *two* sphinxes, both crowned with plumed headdresses. But, others ask, if he is a god, why does he have the hairstyle normally depicted in Cretan art as belonging to a priestess?

And so it goes on. Clearly the representation as it stands is wrong in just about every way it could be. The only thing they got right was the lilies. This may not amount to fraud, but it is certainly a long-sustained deception. Does it really matter? In the course of the century since he was put together, the prince has taken on symbolic force. The fresco is a false image that exposure to millions of people has made true, embedded in popular imagination as the essential expression of Minoan elegance and vivacity of spirit. The original is still on display, among the most treasured possessions of the museum; and a copy still stands under the portico of the south entrance to the palace of Knossos where Evans placed it in 1901, a potent proof—if we needed another—of the power of the image to transcend objective categories of truth and falsehood.

CHAPTER SIX

PEACE AMID

the CLAMOR

East of Iraklion lies the fourth province of Crete, Lasithi, with a high plateau at the heart of it and the sweep of Mirabello Bay as its open face, sheltered to the north by the headland of Agios Ioannis.

Mountain plains—like caves and gorges—are a special feature of Crete; the island numbers dozens or scores or hundreds, depending on the limits of dimension one sets on them. But the Lasithi Plateau is the biggest of them—the biggest flat area on the island. It forms a rough oval, rising to three thousand feet above sea level, eleven and a half square miles in area, entirely surrounded by higher mountains, dotted with thousands of stone windmills installed by the Venetians to irrigate the plain. These are picturesque with their cloth sails and they attract many visitors, but much of the work is done nowadays by gas-driven pumps. It is a fertile region, producing fruit and vegetables in abundance. Even if the windmills have mainly fallen into disuse, the plateau is worth the tortuous fifteen miles of road from Neapoli for the spectacular views, for the experience of an agrarian economy which is, taken acre for acre, one of the most productive anywhere to found.

The vast majority of visitors to the Lasithi Plateau come by bus and stay only for the middle hours of the day. The onslaught is heavy for such a small area, but by early evening almost everyone has left again, and the villages that surround the plateau continue the patterns of traditional life. The influx is contained and released, inhaled and exhaled, like breathing. The rhythms of local existence are disturbed, no doubt, but not much damaged. This is unfortunately not the case with some of the beach resorts to the north. The outskirts of Elounda, on the western side of Mirabello Bay, provide some of the worst examples on the island of the unbridled and haphazard building that has taken place in the rush to get in on the tourist boom.

Negotiating a succession of hairpin bends on the narrow road up to the hotel, we saw a car, victim of an accident, left at the roadside. There was always a damaged car in that same spot, all through the time of our stay there, but the truly alarming thing was that the cars kept changing. Taking this as evidence of frequent collisions on this road, we attempted to use a bus. There was a sort of agreement—or so we understood—between the hotel and the bus company that buses would stop near the hotel to pick up guests. But the drivers seemed unaware of this agreement and went sailing past, so we had to trudge back to the hotel and use the car after all.

This was a minor irritation. But we were both appalled by what had been done to the place itself. For years now an incessant, piecemeal building of vacation accommodations has been going on here, without regard to the rights of access to the coastal hillsides and the shore itself. A great deal of money has gone into this, both public and private, but very little has been invested in projects less immediately profitable, like communications, public transport, services generally. The roads, which are among the busiest in the region, are more or less what they always were, narrow, badly built, and badly surfaced, ever more fume-laden and dangerous. The lower roads, down toward the shore, have been so much encroached upon in the process of building that they are in places too narrow for cars to pass one another without complicated maneuvering, hemmed between the walls of the hotels that stretch ever farther up the hillsides, clambering up like competing plants in a forest, striving for star ratings, a view of the sea.

A dream sea. We had a piece of it to look at from our balcony, or from the poolside. But just try to get there. By and large, there is no way for people staying in these hotels or apartment blocks to explore the locality in which they find themselves. They certainly can't walk anywhere, not with any pleasure. The roads are too harassing and too dangerous. And you can't get off them because everything is staked out and fenced off.

The result of all this, locally around Elounda, as in other places on this north coast of Crete, is truncated hillsides partitioned off into lots, little tracts of no-man's-land awaiting the developer, the occasional acre or two of weeds and shrub, then perhaps a small olive grove that someone still clings to, fenced around with barbed wire. Dotted here and there are gaunt, unfinished buildings, roofless, the concrete framework a dark gray color, awaiting the owner's next burst of prosperity to be converted into yet more vacation accommodations of one sort or another. This uniquely beautiful island, with its long history of human habitation, its landscape at once rugged and mild—the mingling that results from people living in harmony with their surroundings—has had substantial parts of its coastal regions stripped of sense and order in a matter of a few decades.

Not much point now in wondering what combination of greed, ignorance, lack of civic sense, and care for the environment could have led to this state of things. What has been missing is what is always missing, in Crete as in a thousand other places, cooperation between citizen and municipal authority, the ability of local communities, often traditionally poor, to withstand the invasion of capital and so take a longer view, retain some space for human purposes other than the single one of spending money, open the land to people instead of closing it. But this would mean admitting the inadmissible: that constant growth is a chimera, that the stream can dry up, that unlimited numbers of free-spending people cannot be accommodated in a limited space, and that continued attempts to do it will foul up the very thing that the people came for in the first place.

These gloomy thoughts gathered in us but were then dispersed again, dispelled by the sheer, inalienable beauty of the island, which is still, despite all such brutalizing, the truth of it. There is the light, first and foremost. Even the ravaged hillsides of Elounda can seem healed and restored by the benediction of Cretan sunlight. At the changing of the seasons, spring into summer and summer into autumn, there are days of quick transition from overcast skies to periods of clear weather, with extraordinary effects of contrast in the quality of vision. The haze shifts and for some moments everything is seen in a shaft of brilliant light, every slightest gradation of color in the sea, every detail of the horizon, all clear to the point of hallucination. Looking east from Elounda you see the small island of Psira, far out in the bay, suddenly distinct as if someone had snatched away a veil from it, while the headland of Mohlos beyond is still shrouded in a pale violet haze, only just discernible, with the most tenuous of dividing lines between sea and landmass and sky. In this weather the moon goes through spectral changes, at first dark red as it clears the cliffs, then gold, then white as it climbs free of the haze.

And then there is the abiding fact that a little effort will take you clear of crowds into places where you can feel the spell of solitude. A journey of three miles north from the clutter of Elounda, following the coast road toward the tip of the Agios Ioannis headland, brings you to the tranquil resort of Plaka, with its pebbled beach, translucent sea, and tavernas fronting the shore, with fresh fish on offer. Quitting the road and taking the track that leads farther north along the hillside, just above the sea, we found ourselves after ten minutes quite alone. We also found ourselves embarked on a very memorable walk.

No habitations here, no cars—and on the day we did this walk no people, except a young Finnish couple who were setting out along the track as we returned. It is very rare to find a Cretan walking for pleasure. It seems to them a meaningless and redundant activity, perhaps even slightly mad.

The only sounds on this summer day were birdsong and, at first, distant voices from across the water, where boatloads of people were landing on the island fortress of Spinalonga, just beyond the humped promontory below us, which bears the same name. This small island has had a checkered and in some ways chilling history, though it has also been the scene of a moving and courageous human enterprise practically without parallel elsewhere.

The Venetians had already been masters of Crete for more than three hundred years when they decided to fortify the island to guard the approaches to the western side of the gulf and the sheltered anchorages south of the promontory. The remains of the fortress they built are extensive and well preserved, though much overgrown and hazardous to explore. The high walls on the north side, with their crenellations and escarpments— clearly visible to us from the track we were following high above—are cunningly incorporated into the granite of which the island is made. The whole construction is an astonishing feat of engineering. The island was virtually impregnable, and even after the Turkish conquest of Crete in 1669 it did not fall into their hands for another half century—not until 1715. And even then it was not taken by force but ceded by treaty.

Starting with the few Ottoman troops left as a garrison, the population grew until by the end of the nineteenth century more than a thousand families of Turkish descent were living on the island, all of them devoted to the thriving local industry of smuggling. This was so lucrative that even after 1898, when Crete was declared autonomous, the Turks of Spinalonga refused to leave their homes. In 1903, however, they fled en masse when the Cretan Republic under Prince George decided to make the island a leper colony. The story of this colony has been well related by Beryl Darby, and I am indebted to her for many of the details that follow.

Leprosy was still at that time one of the most feared of human diseases, because of its contagiousness, the terrible disfigurements it brought about, the progressive degeneration of the body that accompanied it. And because it was so feared, those who suffered from it were treated as outcasts. Several hundred lepers, men and women, were taken from the caves and shacks where they had been living, all over Crete, and brought here. In these early years, isolated on the island, they were in desperate straits, neglected and abandoned, often in great pain, obliged to fend for themselves without medical attention or regular supplies of food and fresh water, unable to treat the suppurating wounds which are characteristic of the disease. All looked peaceful below us that day: the glittering expanse of the bay, the ferries plying across from Agios Nikolaos and Elounda. But if that little island could voice its own past, the voice would come as a single cry of suffering.

As the century advanced, things got better. A new contingent of lepers was sent to Spinalonga from Athens, people on the whole better educated, less resigned—they numbered lawyers and teachers among them. With the help of the lepers already there, they struggled to establish a community, repairing the dilapidated houses vacated by the Turks, quarrying their own stone to do it. They constructed cisterns to collect rainwater and used the open fireplaces in the old Turkish laundry to heat the water so they could keep their sores clean. They printed their own newspaper, with news of various events on the island. They even built a theater and put on plays. Above all, they assumed responsibility for one another, the stronger attending to the weaker, making sure that no one died alone. It is a story of courage and cooperation under the most terrible conditions and should have pride of place in the annals of heroism.

The last lepers on Spinalonga—the thirty still alive—were transferred to mainland hospitals in 1957. It is a strange experience now to walk about on the island among the decaying houses of the lepers and the scattered ruins of the fort, where the garrisons of the conquerors and the community of the sick once lived and died. This is only a ghost town, with rotting timbers and listing walls and hanging shutters. Some signs of those former lives still remain. The lepers' disinfection room and dispensary are still there, and there are some marks of domestic life: an old basket on a shelf, a tilted cupboard with doors hanging open, a bank of red geraniums growing over a doorway.

The track ascended, Spinalonga was left behind, the bay of Mirabello opened before us, with the mountainous headlands one beyond the other, stretching away east toward Sitia. On the landward side, the hills rose steeply, marked by the dark green of the carob trees, with their lighter clustering pods, and flowering phrygana plants in domed clumps and granite outcrops weathered here and there to a warm red-brown. The mid-morning sun brought out waves of scent, at times almost dizzying, from the aromatic scrub all around us. One can range at will in the Cretan maquis—no venomous snakes lurk here, or anywhere else on the island, which is a very agreeable piece of knowledge for the walker, who has enough to do avoiding the spiny plants that grow everywhere. It seems that there never have been fanged snakes on Crete. Their absence, typically enough, has been explained by stories. In antiquity Herakles was said to have banished them; later this feat was attributed to St. Paul the Apostle, who was bitten by a snake—on Crete, the Cretans say, wanting their island to be the scene of everything, even of disasters; but it was on Malta that it seems to have happened.

Perhaps to make up for this deficiency in the element of danger, a body of folklore has grown up around a lizard of snakelike appearance called *liakoni,* which, though entirely harmless, is still commonly believed by the country people to have a life-threatening bite. In fact, the only really dangerous customer on the island is the Mediterranean black widow spider, recognizable by its black and hairy abdomen, a piece of information I owe to the excellent Natural History Museum of Iraklion. I have never encountered this spider in the flesh, and I hope this lack of acquaintance will long continue.

We walked on and the solitude settled around us. This, in its peace and tranquility, in the heat-hazed shapes of mountains across the bay and the melting line of the horizon where sea meets sky with a blue that belongs to neither, this is among the most beautiful places our Earth has to show. We found ourselves fervently hoping that it would be left alone for anyone to enjoy, that people were not sitting in some office at that very moment, making dire plans to develop it.

The light is so extraordinary—one keeps coming back to that. It is soft and radiant yet at the same time relentlessly clear. Cretans on the whole, like their compatriots on the mainland, have not been much given to folktales of the darker sort, those featuring threatened children and ambiguous adults liable to change masks. The light here is too clear and bold for such a tradition to develop. You need the more diffused light and more enveloping shadow of northern latitudes for that. There is in Crete, of course, as all over Greece, a prevalent belief in the evil eye, and this is certainly an ambiguous matter, because anyone can have it and exercise it without in the least being aware, conscious of nothing but goodwill. On the other hand, there are those believed to possess this power and to use it malignantly and in secret. At least until recently—and perhaps still today—it was not uncommon for the village priest to be called in to expel demonic presences and purify the house. Blue beads are often used as talismans, worn about the person or hung up in a car, to ward off evil influences of this kind. Sometimes, when people have misfortunes not easy to explain in the natural course of events, they carry out tests to try to determine whether the evil eye is at work. Once I was present at such a test. It consisted of adding drops of olive oil to a glass of water: If the oil floated, which of course it should normally do, all was well; if it mingled with the water, demons were at work. This time, to everyone's relief, the oil conformed to the laws of its nature and floated. On another occasion I was suspected of having the evil eye myself. I was giving a hand with harvesting the grapes in the vineyard of some neighbors. It started to rain in the middle of the morning and went on for two or three hours—a very unusual event for the time of year. Grapes should never be harvested wet; the skins break too easily and there is danger of mold. I was the newcomer, the stranger. It was obvious that I had brought bad luck, and behind bad luck is always the possibility of the evil eye. I was asked, politely but with unmistakable firmness, not to offer my services the next day. And sure enough, the next day it didn't rain.

We kept to the track, gradually climbing, following the curving line of the hillside, with the shimmering expanse of the water below, coming eventually to the narrow tip of the promontory. Here, fitting end to such a walk, lest there should be danger of beauty saturation, a huge fence barred the way, sixteen feet high at least, surmounted by six rows of barbed wire and an enormous circular sign that read: STOP. Only the military can make their meaning as crystal clear as this. From here, if you could get through, you would find yourself looking out toward the Sporades, with Turkey, the traditional foe, beyond.

The track continued around the headland, leading to the road that runs south again toward the village of Vrouhas. But we wanted those views again and so retraced our steps. Coming from this side we noticed what we had missed before: At roughly the halfway mark was a cave above the track, the entrance walled very carefully with close-fitting stones to a height of about five feet. The wall blocked the entrance completely—there was no way in without climbing over it. Inside was a flat area, just enough space for a man to stretch out.

Caves are always a mystery. Who had laid stone on stone to build this wall, now peacefully colonized by purple campanula growing along its base? Fugitive, hermit, guerilla? Xan Fielding, who had more firsthand experience of Cretan caves than most, having fought in the White Mountains with the Resistance during the years of German occupation, relates a story that perfectly illustrates the Cretan desire to appropriate the past, to be the source of things, to blend myth and history into a possession as real and solid as the stones of their island.

While Fielding was sheltering in a cave near Souyia in 1942, a local man told him that the cave he was inhabiting was the very one in which the Cyclops Polyphemus once lived and kept his flocks. The Cyclops were a savage race of one-eyed giants who lived by tending sheep. Homer tells the story of how Odysseus and his companions, returning from Troy, took shelter in the cave of Polyphemus, who, finding them there, began systematically to eat them. He had already devoured six when they disabled him by driving a fire-hardened stake into his single eye while he lay sleeping. The blinded giant pushed aside the huge stone that blocked the entrance and kept his sheep penned in the cave. He tried to fumble for his enemies as they went through, but they clung to the fleecy undersides of the sheep and so got free. Once embarked again, Odysseus could not resist taunting his outwitted enemy. The enraged Polyphemus cast down great rocks in the direction of the voice, almost succeeding in crushing Odysseus's ship. The giant's prayers for vengeance to his father Poseidon roused the sea god's wrath against Odysseus and cost the hero ten years of troubles and dangers before he could return to his native Ithaka and his faithful Queen Penelope.

It happened here, Fielding's Cretan friend insisted, this was the cave. And to prove it he pointed out two rocks in the sea below. Those were the stones that the stricken monster hurled down. The commonly accepted view, which sets the scene off the Sicilian coast near Catania, was quite mistaken. The story belonged to Crete and it had been stolen from her.

This stubborn sense of possession is not surprising when one considers Crete's history. Foreign masters, alien religions, these were the Cretans' familiar circumstances for many hundreds of years, and the refusal to submit, the frequent uprisings, cost the people untold bloodshed and suffering. In these circumstances, whatever can serve to maintain the spirit and sense of identity must be seized upon and asserted. In Cretan folk song, and especially the *rizitika,* the mountain songs that began to appear in the eighteenth century during the darkest days of the Turkish occupation, two themes occur again and again: the beauty of the island and the indomitable spirit of its people. This is entirely to be expected. If you are called upon to suffer in defense of something, whether a land or ideal—and in this case it was both—it is natural to stress the desirability of what you are defending and the courage needed to defend it.

There have been other by-products of occupation. The Cretans, like the Greeks generally, have always been characterized by an inability to combine together and present a common front. Never was that saying of Terence truer of any people: "So many men, so many

opinions: each a law unto himself." The spirit of resistance, even to a common enemy, and the harshness of the
struggle, instead of uniting the people, seems to have
led to that fierce kind of individualism and independence that lays stress on narrowly local loyalties.

Then there is what seems to many foreign observers
the strongly materialistic view of life that most Cretans
take. If you see a group of men in earnest conversation
in a bar, they are quite likely to be talking about the
cost of living. Any vague and unfounded rumor of a
bread shortage on the way can result in panic buying
and hoarding on a large scale. This is not the kind of
consumerism that characterizes more prosperous societies
in the West; it is more like a fear of want, of being left
unprotected. Generalizations are dangerous, we all know
that, but it doesn't seem too fanciful to set this down,
at least to a considerable extent, to the insecurities of
countless former generations still working in the psyche
of the people.

These were the thoughts set in train by that metic-
ulously walled cave that we saw on our way back to
Plaka. We never succeeded in finding out anything
more about this, either because those we asked didn't
know, or because my Greek was not really up to it....

Principal town on the Bay of Mirabello, and capital
of the province of Lasithi, is Agios Nikolaos, which has

a cosmopolitan feel, reflected in the bars and restaurants and in the general style of life—it probably has the highest concentration of resident expatriates anywhere in Crete. The setting is striking: The town is built on a small peninsula around a lake of darkly shining water, described as bottomless in the tourist literature and even on street signs. Certainly it is very deep—seventy-five feet, I was told, at the deepest point. The lake has an outlet to the sea and so forms an inner harbor. Some of the lakeside restaurants are excellent, more sophisticated and offering a wider choice than is general on the island, with very good pasta dishes on the menu and imaginative salads and specialties like grilled swordfish or zucchini flowers fried in an egg batter, accompanied by the light, dry Cretan wines, so much pleasanter—to my taste, at least—than the resinated wine called retsina, common on the Greek mainland. Cretan red wines have always been well thought of by visitors and inhabitants alike, but the white have improved very considerably in the last ten years or so, especially those from the region of Sitia.

The town beaches can scarcely be called beaches at all, but we found a good one at Almiros, just a little over a mile to the south. Farther around the bay, in the area of Kalo Chorio, they get better and better. My own favorite is Istro, which has pleasant tavernas and some excellent sandy beaches; in places they have even spared the trees lying back from the shore. From here, I think better than anywhere else on the island, you can enjoy the combined beach and sight-seeing holiday that brings so many people to Crete. For those who like walking, tracks in the hills behind afford splendid views over the bay. Knossos is not far away, perhaps an hour by road. Nearer at hand is Gournia, another Minoan palace site, spectacularly situated on a saddle between two peaks, from where it once controlled the isthmus between the north and south coasts, no more than twelve miles at this narrowest point.

The Church of Panagia Kira near the village of Kritsa, a little way inland from Istro, is one of the loveliest of Byzantine churches and one of the oldest, with the most complete set of frescoes to be found on Crete, painted at different times in the island's history and thus affording a unique opportunity to trace the developing styles of Cretan fresco painting through the fourteenth and fifteenth centuries. Among a number of paintings of outstanding quality and interest is a tremendous Last Supper in the center, and in the southern aisle vivid scenes of Christ's Second Coming, including representations of the Day of Judgment and the Punishment of the Damned. On the northwestern pillar is a portrayal of St. Francis of Assisi—a very rare instance of a Western saint in an Orthodox church,

The Church of Panagia Kira, near Kritsa

perhaps the result of Venetian influence. Crete is well endowed with churches, many of them beautifully situated and full of interest; but if obliged to choose among them, to single out one which best exemplifies the atmosphere and the spirit of devotion of medieval Byzantium, I would favor the Panagia Kira.

The days were running out now, they had gone quickly. We had started wondering—always a sign that a trip is coming to an end—how things were at home, whether our vines and olives were prospering, whether there had been enough rain. We would have the grass to cut and the aphids to deal with and the vegetable garden to clear of weeds. We would have to secure the forgiveness of our five cats for having stayed away so long....

There was still so much left to see. We decided to continue south across the neck of the isthmus to Ierapetra, which is the largest town on the south coast, the hottest and driest town on the island, and the southernmost town in Europe. But our desire to go there didn't stem so much from statistics, though these do in a way affect one's attitude to places. We had talked ourselves into a valedictory mood, and it seemed somehow fitting to end our trip in the region where the last descendents of the Minoan people, whose history of power and decline had so absorbed us as we went from room to room in the Iraklion museum, met their end. They are known as Eteocretans, or "true Cretans," people of the original, pre-Greek stock. They had been driven to this remote eastern region of the island, where they preserved themselves for some centuries in their fortified city of Presos, still clinging to their language and traditional mode of life. They were finally defeated in 146 B.C. by the Dorians of Ierapetra. Those who were not killed or sold into the slavery were scattered and ceased to be a separate component of the population. Their city was razed to the ground. Thus ended what has been called the thousand-year twilight of Minoan civilizations.

Of ancient Presos little remains now—it was never rebuilt. Present-day Ierapetra is a prosperous town with a handsome waterfront and a very good beach. May was advanced, we were about to return to landlocked Umbria, so we ventured in for a swim. The water was chilly, but—as people say when they are glad to get out again—invigorating.

By this time we were both feeling hungry, but we wanted to have our lunch somewhere quiet—Ierapetra seemed too busy and townish. We got into the car again and headed westward. The road keeps close to the coast for seven or eight miles, then turns sharply inland. Just below where this change of direction occurs is the village of Mirtos, an altogether captivating seaside resort with the tremendous advantage of being at the end of a turnoff from the main road, which passes well above it, so there is a blessed absence of traffic, creating an air of leisure and tranquility that is increasingly rare in Cretan coastal resorts. There was a long, curving shingle beach and a promenade running close to the water, lined with bars and tavernas. The houses were whitewashed and scrupulously clean and neat. There were no very old-looking buildings anywhere in evidence, also unusual but not surprising in view of what we had read of the wartime history of the village: Mirtos was destroyed by the Germans in 1943 in reprisal for resistance activities.

The job was done thoroughly; it seems they hardly left one stone on top of another. But Mirtos, unlike the last refuge of the Eteocretans, was rebuilt.

Tastes differ, in places as in most other things; and as we know, it is useless to argue about them. Often enough it is what the place stands for as much as what it is in itself that draws our regard or rouses our affection. I took to Mirtos immediately, not only because it is peaceful and pretty—there are still quite a lot of places on the island that fit this description—but because it has been terribly mistreated in the past, and yet has restored and renewed itself. And so it comes to represent what I feel about the history and the spirit of Crete as a whole.

At Mirtos, sitting at an outside table of the Votsalo tavern, with the sea just below and a warm breeze wafting over from Africa, glasses of the excellent Greek Mythos beer at our elbows and the resident cats showing great interest in our mutton chops, we had to start thinking about getting back to Iraklion and then home to Italy. The trip had been a success for both of us, in slightly different ways. For Aira, seeing the island for the first time and adding it to her list of places to see again. And for me, seeing it again and finding it essentially as I remembered. To leave them always with regret is the gift some places—not so many—make us. It's the gift life itself makes us, if we are lucky.

BIBLIOGRAPHY

Leonard Cottrell
The Bull of Minos (London, 1953)

Costis Davaras
Guide to Cretan Antiquities (Athens, 1976)

Xan Fielding
The Stronghold (London, 1953)

Mihalis G. Andrianakis
The Holy Patriarchal Monastery of Agia Triada (Chania, 1994)

Nikos Psilakis
Byzantine Churches and Monasteries of Crete (Iraklion, 1994)

Oliver Rackham and Jennifer Moody
The Making of the Cretan Landscape (Manchester University Press, 1996)

Adam Hopkins
Crete: Its Past, Present & People (London, 1977)

John Fisher and Geoff Garvey
The Rough Guide: Crete (Fourth Edition, London, 1998)

Michael Llewellyn Smith
The Great Island (London, 1965)

Theocharis E. Detorakis
History of Crete (Iraklion, 1994)

Sonia Greger
Letters from Lasithi 1984–1993 (Gorgona Books, 1993)

Joan Evans
Time and Chance (London, 1943)

Beryl Darby
Spinalonga: The Leper Island (Athens, 2001)

J. D. S. Pendlebury
A Handbook to the Palace of Minos at Knossos (London, 1932)

ABOUT THE AUTHOR

Barry Unsworth won the Booker Prize in 1992 for *Sacred Hunger;* his next novel, *Morality Play,* was a Booker nominee and a bestseller both in the United States and in Great Britain. His other novels include *Pascali's Island, After Hannibal, The Hide, Losing Nelson,* and *The Songs of the Kings.* He lives in Umbria, Italy, with his wife, Aira.

This book is set in Garamond 3, designed by
Morris Fuller Benton and Thomas Maitland
Cleland in the 1930s, and Lithos, inspired
by Greek inscriptional letters from the fourth
century B.C., designed by Carol Twombly.
Both are released digitally by Adobe.

Printed by R. R. Donnelley and Sons on
Gladfelter 60-pound Thor Offset smooth
white antique paper.

Dust jacket printed by Miken Companies.
Color separation by Quad Graphics.

Three-piece case of Ecological Fiber black side
panels with Sierra black book cloth as the spine
fabric. Stamped in Lustrofoil metallic silver.

NATIONAL GEOGRAPHIC DIRECTIONS

Featuring works by some of the world's most prominent and highly regarded literary figures, National
Geographic Directions captures the spirit of travel
and of place for which National Geographic is
renowned, bringing fresh perspective and renewed
excitement to the art of travel writing.